NO BAD DAYS

WORKBOOK

SEIZE YOUR OPPORTUNITY

DR. KAROCKAS "DOC ROCK" WATKINS

No Bad Days Workbook
by Dr. Karockas Watkins
© 2024 by Dr. Karockas Watkins. All rights reserved.

Editing by Adam Colwell's WriteWorks, LLC, Adam Colwell and Ginger Colwell
Cover and interior design by Clarity Designworks
Published by Dr. Karockas Watkins through IngramSpark
Printed in the United States of America
ISBN (Paperback): 979-8-9914678-0-3

While the author has made every effort to provide accurate internet addresses at the time of publication, neither the publisher nor the author assumes any responsibility for errors or for changes that occur after publication. Further, the publisher does not have any control over and does not assume any responsibility for author or third-party websites or their content.

All accounts from Dr. Karockas Watkins' life experiences are non-fiction. All other stories featured throughout this workbook are ficticious accounts based on actual experiences and events. Any resemblance to real persons or ficticious characters, dead or alive, or other real-life of ficticious entities, past or present, is entirely coincidental.

CONTENTS

EVERY DAY MATTERS!

Do you wake up and wonder how the day is going to go? It is easy to accept the _____ expectation for small or average results. You may allow little things to stop you from achieving your best in a given day. At the same time, there are people who seem to be offended, and think you positively strange, when you have an overly _____ disposition.

Writer Edmond Mbiaka is quoted as saying, "Every single day is a good day, no matter how bright or dark it is, because it always brings an opportunity to start a positive beginning in your life." Your day is not to be shaped by the _____ things that happen as it progresses, but by the _____ vision you have as you go about that day.

NATHAN'S STORY

A fan of Edmond Mbiaka's proliferation of inspirational quotes published online and in books, Nathan was nevertheless struggling with his outlook on life. A rookie firefighter, Nathan was coming off a divorce and was overwhelmed at times from the pressures of his new profession and the transition in his personal life. It was hard to find balance and contentment. Then he read Mbiaka's insights about daily living. It said that an unhappy man tends to view happiness as a mystery. So, he walks from coast to coast and swims from shore to shore searching for it, but after so many frustrating attempts, he gives up on it and says to himself that happiness is definitely an impossible task to achieve. Therefore, he settles with his painful misery believing it is an unchangeable way of life.

However, Mbiaka continued, a wise man sees happiness as a matter of deciding to focus on the positive side of his experiences in life rather than giving his negative experiences the permission to hold his mind in an everlasting bondage of misery. "Happiness doesn't rely on your circumstances in life," Mbiaka wrote. "Rather, its existence lies on your positive interpretations of all your circumstances in life."

The truth of Mbiaka's words made Nathan realize that he couldn't continue pushing away or denying his problems. Instead, he had to deal with them from an optimistic mindset. Another one of Mbiaka's quotes came to mind. "A person's thoughts have far more control of one's destiny than the person's enemies do."

That night, Nathan had dinner with his friend, John. Nathan told him what he'd read that day, then said, "I think that good people will make the right choice when it really matters." Since then, Nathan has done just that—facing his challenges and making decisions one day at a time, seeing each day as the opportunity that it is.

Questions for application:

1. Nathan saw himself as being overwhelmed, leaving him discontented. What thought continues to repeat itself in your mind and control your destiny?

_____

_____

_____

_____

_____

2. Investigate a truth that can counter that thought. Write it down here.

_____

_____

_____

_____

_____

3. What opportunities lie in front of you today? List two.

_____

_____

Oftentimes, the things that make up your day are a byproduct of your understanding and inner thoughts.

I acted upon this truth when I found myself in a new executive position at a large not-for-profit organization. We went through a major period of transition, and they were challenging times. As I found myself struggling with motivation for myself and for my management team—I decided to do something about it.

Inspired by the biblical exhortations in Philippians 4, I began telling myself one thing at the start of every day.

There are no bad days.

Before you proceed, write down the first thought you have in response to the statement, "There are no bad days."

_____

_____

_____

_____

_____

As a Christian, I believed that God created each day to live to my fullest. I knew God wanted me to rejoice and be glad about the _____ that came with each day. So, from that moment forward, I chose to never give in to disappointment and be sorry for an entire day.

Then I matched my attitude with a response. I gave each day a special name that I call, sign, and profess. For example, I call Sunday "Super Sunday." I sign it by using "Super Sunday" in my electronic messages. I profess it by saying "It's a Super Sunday" aloud throughout the day.

I also came up with the following:

- Marvelous Monday
- Terrific Tuesday
- Wonderful Wednesday
- Triumphant Thursday
- Fantastic Friday
- Successful Saturday

To be honest, these started out as nothing more than titles, but I have since developed attributes, characteristics, and principles to go with each one. At the foundation of *No Bad Days* is the idea of **self-motivation**, which I define as the ability to _____ yourself to do what needs to be done without influence from other people.

Look again at your initial response to, "There are no bad days." How can you motivate yourself beyond that thought to stir yourself to a more positive outlook for your future?

_____

_____

_____

_____

_____

I recall a time when many of my company's managers were settling for merely meeting industry standards for how we serve our clients: middle-aged men and women with some sort of intellectual disability. I wanted us to do more than simply engage our clients to learn.

So, I took it upon myself to reach deep within and challenge all of us to come up with new approaches that took existing industry standards to a whole new level. We brought in people to teach art and music therapy. We started an entrepreneurship program where our clients could discover how to maximize their gifts. We found out their passions and worked on how we could help them perfect those passions. We even changed the branding of the company to indicate the extra level of services we were providing. In no time, our company *became* the industry leader in our field. More than that, our clients' lives were being enhanced.

1. When was the last time you reached "deep within" to meet a challenge in your life? What was the outcome?

_____

_____

_____

_____

_____

2. What did that experience teach you about self-motivation?

_____

_____

_____

_____

_____

Another word for self-motivation is **intrinsic motivation**. Intrinsic motivation involves engaging in a behavior because it is personally rewarding, enjoyable, or interesting, doing it for *its own sake* rather than from some external pressure or for an external reward. The _____ itself is its own reward.

It's been said that basketball legend Michael Jordan never played against others, but against himself. He was intrinsically motivated, and that motivation led him to become what many consider to be the greatest basketball player of all time. A practical example of intrinsic motivation is taking on more responsibility at work because you want to be challenged, and you enjoy the feeling of accomplishment it brings, rather than doing it to get a raise or a promotion. Another example is learning a new language because you like experiencing new things, not because your job requires it.

MELISSA'S STORY

When Melissa first came across Tamara, the teenage girl was homeless and sleeping in the backseat of an old Datsun 280Z. After learning that Tamara's parents were deceased and that she had run away from violent relatives, Melissa befriended Tamara. Despite being in a demanding job, Melissa helped Tamara any way she could, including allowing the girl to temporarily stay with her in her apartment. Melissa also assisted Tamara with her homework assignments and with finding employment.

Melissa was intrinsically motivated throughout her relationship with Tamara. Not only was it personally rewarding, but she had a good time with Tamara and found her life, particularly her studies, to be unusual and intriguing. No one told Melissa to help Tamara. She received no accolades for her involvement with the girl. Melissa did it simply because she wanted to—and she still treasures those few years of interconnection with Tamara and the influence she had in the girl's life.

Questions for application:

1. Share the story of a time you were intrinsically motivated to do something.

   _____

   _____

   _____

   _____

2. Did you find the experience to be personally rewarding, enjoyable, or interesting?

   _____

   _____

   _____

   _____

3. What is your enduring feeling of accomplishment from that experience?

   _____

   _____

   _____

   _____

Essential to developing your intrinsic motivation is knowing your "why." In my books *God-A-Tude* and *Attitude Determines Altitude*, I talk about your why as being the _____ you exist—your purpose for living. I tell people that their why is that thing that will get them out of bed when everyone else is still hitting the snooze button. When you discover your why, you will search diligently to recognize how to accomplish it, and you will wait as long as it takes to gain the knowledge, stability, and experience to fulfill it.

Your why shouldn't be something that is done just for money, because when you find your passion and it informs your purpose, you'll never "work" a day in your life.

1. What is your passion?

   _____

   _____

   _____

   _____

   _____

2. What comes easily to you?

   _____

   _____

   _____

   _____

   _____

3. What excites you?

   _____

   _____

   _____

   _____

   _____

4. What do your answers to the previous three questions tell you about your why—the passion that informs your purpose?

   _____

   _____

   _____

   _____

   _____

Another key to your intrinsic motivation is having a circle of safety. You will function better, and innovation will be stirred within you, when you are in a safe environment. Your circle of safety also serves as your accountability group, allowing you to get up each morning, dream, and be motivated to take chances because you know that if you fail, your group will not judge you according to that failure.

Do you have a "circle of safety" in your life?   Yes   No

If so, describe it and the purpose it serves.

_____

_____

_____

_____

_____

If not, speculate what you can do to create a safe environment where you will function better and be innovative.

I've identified seven factors of intrinsic motivation.

1. **Curiosity** pushes you to _____ and learn for the sole pleasure of learning and mastering. In her article, "The Importance of Being Curious," leadership expert Dalia Molokhia shares about how being curious by putting herself in her young daughters' shoes as she learned new things has helped her as a mother. When you are curious, you open yourself to new information. In his Harvard Business Review article, "Why Curious People Are Destined for the C-Suite," Warren Berger told of the time when Dell Technologies founder, chairman, and CEO Michael Dell was asked in a PwC survey to name a trait that would most help chief executive officers succeed. Dell's response: "I would place my bet on curiosity."

Name something that you're curious about that you've yet to learn or pursue.

_____

_____

_____

_____

_____

2. Being **challenged** helps you work at a continuously _____ level toward meaningful goals to maximize your potential. As a CEO, I was once challenged, during an executive board meeting, with an aggressive goal to increase the number of clients we serve by three times more than the industry standard. The colleague said, "Doc Rock, I feel you and your team can do much more than this." Even though the colleague was a friend, it felt like an attack and one where I was being set up for failure. After gathering myself and realizing that he was challenging me to go beyond what I thought I could do, I asked myself, "Why am I looking to industry criteria to define what I can and can't do? I *can* do better, so let me be who I know I am." Within a year, we not only met the goal, but exceeded the industry standard for new client acquisitions by almost five times the amount.

Do you enjoy being challenged? Why or why not?

_____

_____

_____

_____

_____

3. **Control** comes from your basic desire to _____ what happens and make decisions that affect the outcome. There was an executive who had to take control of a very politicized situation facing his company regarding cultural diversity. Disunity and strife within the community that the organization served was having a detrimental impact on many business leaders and their stakeholders. It resulted in some heated exchanges around the boardroom table, but the executive proactively worked to help everyone to see beyond their personal opinions and prejudices and to look at the situation in a positive manner. As a result, the leadership team was able to determine a proper organizational response, and everyone was motivated to stay the course.

Describe a time in the past year when you had an impact on someone or something that had a positive outcome.

_____

_____

_____

_____

_____

4. You possess an innate need to be **complimented** and to see that you are _____ and that your efforts are confirmed. Some people act as if they don't need to be complimented, but it is helpful, if only for the purpose of motivation. One of my dear colleagues who is a self-starter and a very disciplined person once admitted that while he was in college, he felt much better after he was complimented on the work he was doing as president of one of the student body clubs. He said the compliment served as additional fuel to fire his success by helping him accomplish more than he would have without the encouragement.

    What was the last compliment you received? How has it helped you?

    _____

    _____

    _____

    _____

    _____

5. **Cooperating** with others satisfies your need for _____. You also feel personal satisfaction when you help others and work together with them to achieve a shared goal. While serving on a board for a local branch of the YMCA (Young Men's Christian Association), I worked with the executive director on his vision and goals for the branch. We talked to potential donors together and formed several strategies, and it felt absolutely great to team up with such a talented individual. Not only did he encourage me, but he offered a higher level of insight that told me we couldn't do it alone and that we were better together. It is not about taking credit or having your name out there. It is about the cooperation of a team that satisfies your need to belong.

    Share the story of a recent time you felt like you belonged to something bigger than yourself.

    _____

    _____

    _____

    _____

    _____

6. **Competition** poses a challenge and increases the _____ you place on doing well. There was a time that I had two mid-level managers who were in competition for a new position we were creating in the company. Both came to me requesting to compete for the opening so that they could be motivated to rise to their best leadership skills and behavior. So, I went and observed them as they worked with individuals within their current departments, had meetings, and set goals. I gave them a level playing field, and the competition between the two was friendly yet determined. In the end, one rose to the top, but both learned, grew, and thrived. It was a really good process.

Do you enjoy being competitive? Why or why not?

_____

_____

_____

_____

_____

7. Using the **canvas** of your imagination _____ your behavior as you use it to draw upon mental or virtual images. I have always said that if you can see something on the canvas of your imagination, you can have it! I discovered this to be true for myself when our company faced a difficult season. Everything looked bleak and problematic, but I had to visualize us doing well and becoming a great company within our industry. When I got to the office each day, I had some quiet time in which I pictured us succeeding, responding to crises, and being financially sound. I envisioned us talking to our clients so that they became partners with us. I saw us with smiles on our faces and receiving awards for our work. I told everyone what I saw and what I believed we could be, then we had meetings on how we could get there and put strategies in place to make things happen.

Within just two weeks, things started to change, and in six months, we had everything turned around! Visualizing was the initial dynamic, then my actions toward my team, as well as toward my own responsibilities, began to manifest what I was visualizing.

Use the space below to draw an aspiration you've created on the canvas of your imagination. Don't worry about your artistic ability. Simply show what you saw—and describe the dream it represents.

Of course, self-motivated people are also enthusiastic. They have the ability to complete a task even in the face of barriers.

There was a time at General Motors when I had to assist in the completion of a project with an aggressive two week deadline. My team and I decided to make it a fun challenge. As engineers, we began by encouraging those on the production line to let us help them to troubleshoot the problems and teach us what we missed. "Tomorrow, we are going to be able to test five parts," I said, "then, the next day, we are going to test ten parts. Who is going to be the person who leads the team today?"

No one wanted to let us down. Despite hard work and long hours, our shared enthusiasm drove us to complete the task on deadline and with excellence. It was all a matter of changing our mindset about the task from being an overwhelming and difficult burden to an enjoyable responsibility that we did together. That made the project less daunting and more realistic to execute.

TITUS' STORY

Titus was a criminology student who, in youthful arrogance, considered himself to be somewhat of a subject matter expert. Then he received his score on the mid-term exam and discovered, to his dismay, that it was close to failing. To make matters worse, his instructor, Mr. Grey, gave Titus daily reports to complete until he felt satisfied with Titus' performance. As a result, Titus placed more pressure than ever on himself. He was driven to achieve, but in his eyes, nothing short of perfection was good enough.

In the meantime, Titus' landlord was arrested on drug charges, prompting him to find a new place to live. After looking at a few undesirable options, a classmate, Lucy, came to his rescue and found him an apartment next door to hers. Not long after that, Titus had a severe allergic reaction to an unknown substance he was inadvertently exposed to that resulted in his appearing to be high in class. However, once the cause was identified, Mr. Grey's trust in Titus increased as he saw Titus excel on his daily reports despite the unforeseen circumstances he had to overcome.

Finally, near the close of the semester, Titus had stayed the course and learned some needed humility in the process. He also discovered how to be less demanding of himself. Not only did Titus score well on the final exam, he aced it. Mr. Grey recognized Titus' efforts in front of the entire class, citing his student's mindset change and unwavering enthusiasm as two big reasons why Titus was able to conquer the obstacles he faced.

Questions for application:

1. When did overconfidence or arrogance undermine you at your workplace? Share the story.

_____

_____

_____

_____

_____

2. What mindset changes did you make to properly address the issue?

_____

_____

_____

_____

_____

3. Name one way you now use enthusiasm to stay self-motivated?

_____

_____

_____

_____

_____

Finally, a crucial part of self-motivation is decision making. This can be daunting, and it can pull strongly on your emotions. Making hard decisions is not always easy, and it can be damaging if not properly handled.

There was an occasion when I had to release one of our vice presidents over company administration. This was difficult for me to do because he was close to several other leaders. Out of respect and fairness, I should have met personally with that individual before I allowed the chief operations officer to let him go, explaining why he was being released—but I didn't. He was rightfully angry that I didn't talk to him, and to this day, he is respectful but aloof toward me.

On another front, I oversaw a difficult decision to move our company's payday from every other Friday to every other Monday, knowing it would disturb many team members and possibly cause some to leave the company altogether. To achieve this transition without a major uprising, we decided to give everyone their first pay a week in advance and included extra compensation to cover the anticipated cost of the initial three-day delay. Most everyone saw it as a bonus and got on board with the change. It was a wonderful way to show that we had heard and understood their concerns and needs by giving them a way to plan ahead and adjust their personal expenditures such as paying bills or grocery shopping.

1. Describe a hard decision you had to make in the past month?

_____

_____

_____

_____

_____

2. What was the outcome—and what did you learn about yourself from that outcome?

_____

_____

_____

_____

_____

In the end, every decision you make has consequences—and your decisions today will determine your quality of life tomorrow. Your decisions sculpt your destiny.

With that in mind, *No Bad Days* will teach you how to develop and maintain the mindset required to make the right decisions so that every day matters.

We will explore the attributes of each day. What, exactly, make Sundays super?

We will examine the characteristics of each day. What are the common traits that make Mondays marvelous?

We will learn principles that define how Tuesdays are terrific, Wednesdays are wonderful, and so on.

By the time we're done, you'll never look at the calendar, your schedule—or your life—the same way again.

So, let's begin with what many people see as the first day of the week, even if it isn't the traditional start of the work week.

Every Day Matters **Fill-in-the-Blank Answer Key:**

normal	stir	impact
positive	behavior	appreciated
external	reason	belonging
internal	explore	importance
opportunities	optimal	stimulates

Notes

[1]

SUPER SUNDAY
Vision

Anything super _____ with a vision. I love its American Heritage Dictionary definition. Vision is an unusual competence in discernment of an extraordinarily beautiful thing which you _____ or experience in your mind. Please read that over again. Isn't it telling?

There is no doubt that one of the greatest visions ever expressed to a country and its people was the one Dr. Martin Luther King Jr. discerned of a united America without judgment and racism. The following excerpt, from his speech on the steps of the Lincoln Memorial at The March on Washington for Jobs and Freedom on August 28, 1963, will remain among the most famous words ever spoken.

"So even though we face the difficulties of today and tomorrow, I still have a dream. It is a dream deeply rooted in the American dream. I have a dream that one day this nation will rise up and live out the true meaning of its creed, 'We hold these truths to be self-evident, that all men are created equal.' … I have a dream that my four little children will one day live in a nation where they will not be judged by the color of their skin but by the content of their character."[1]

Think about Dr. King's incredible statement. Using it as inspiration, what is something you can envision happening in your life in the next year? Write down the first thing that comes to your mind.

_____

_____

_____

_____

Yet long before he made that great speech, Dr. King had implemented the Beloved Community, a group of people committed to, and trained in, the philosophy and methods of nonviolence. This was the cornerstone of the principles used by those involved in the civil rights movement of the 1950s-60s. They believed in a global vision where poverty, hunger, and homelessness were not to be tolerated because international standards of decency wouldn't allow it. In this vision, racism and all forms of discrimination and prejudice were to be replaced by an all-inclusive spirit of brotherhood and sisterhood.

Now that's a vision that communicates "an unusual competence in discernment of an extraordinarily beautiful thing." Dr. King saw and experienced this in his mind, and he dedicated his life—and ultimately lost it—doing everything he could to make it a reality.

As it was for Dr. King, so it can be for you. Your vision is *part* of who you _____ and what you are doing or are going to do. *Who* you are is your _____, your reason for existing. Many times, people don't see their purpose, but when it is crafted into a vision, both they and others can see and experience it. No wonder pastor, author, and leadership expert Bill Hybels said, "Vision is a picture of the future that produces passion."

For example, let's say I declare a vision to travel around the world and speak. Then I get more specific, indicating that I want to go to Africa. I begin to talk about going to Africa and believing that things are going to open up for me to do so. That includes speaking with people and describing what I wish to see happen, detailing the countries or cities I wish to visit, what I want to achieve there, and what needs to be accomplished for me to get there. I talk about going to Africa in such a way that others are going to be able to see what I am saying—proclaiming my vision as purpose in picture form as though I was painting it onto a canvas. This results in providing people an opportunity to help fulfill the vision and make it come to pass.

LAUREN'S AND ALEXIS' STORY

As mother and daughter, Lauren and Alexis were inseparable. A divorced mom, Lauren lovingly doted on Alexis, in part to compensate for the absence of her father, but also because she felt Alexis was exceptional. Lauren did everything she could to provide for her family, becoming an entrepreneur in the process, and ensure that Alexis had everything she needed to pursue her dream of opening a coffee bistro with her. They spoke about it, planned for it step-by-step, and told others what they were going to achieve. They even visited other diners and coffee shops in the area so they could better see the bistro they wanted to create in their mind's eyes. It seemed everything was falling into place.

Then Alexis hit a shocking roadblock. An admired professional peer told her she didn't have what it took to succeed as an entrepreneur. The blunt criticism rocked Alexis to her core—so much so that she told her mother she no longer wanted to be a part of the bistro. For the first time in her young life, Alexis gave up.

The next several months were extremely hard on both mother and daughter. For a time, they were even estranged from one another. However, Lauren knew her daughter needed to figure things out on her own. Eventually, after receiving unexpected encouragement from a friend, Alexis regained confidence in herself and her abilities. She cast aside the harsh words of the peer and reconciled with her mother. Her renewed vision became her passion, and Alexis worked with Lauren to open their coffee bistro (featuring their signature "Luke's Roast" served in oversized mugs) two years later. It remains a beloved favorite of their many fans.

Questions for application:

1. Share the story of a time you were told you weren't good enough.

_____

_____

_____

_____

_____

2. How did you respond? Did you briefly give up, did you do something else, or did you follow your original vision? Why?

_____

_____

_____

_____

_____

3. What was the outcome—and what did you learn about your vision in the process?

_____

_____

_____

_____

_____

4. Do you, like Alexis, have someone who is helping you achieve your vision? If so, describe how that person enables you the most.

_____

_____

_____

_____

_____

As you begin discerning the beautiful to create purpose-driven visions that you want to achieve in your life, there are three truths about vision that will guide you in the process.

1. **Vision will put you in over your head (beyond your human capacity), but never beyond your potential, to produce.** When I first started my leadership consultant firm, Vision Excellence Company, I had a vision that I would be teaching before multimillion dollar organizations. That was very much outside of my immediate circles of influence and was over the top of what I had done in the past. But my vision kept me hungry, and that hunger encouraged me to keep studying, learning, and striving for excellence. Within five years, I found myself conducting an Emotional Intelligence seminar at a Christian ministry headquarters in Philadelphia, Pennsylvania—the national hub of a multimillion dollar organization. My vision had been fulfilled. Since then, I've worked with no less than a dozen other companies that size, affirming my continuing potential to achieve the goal I envisioned.

1. Describe a time in the past year when you felt in over your head professionally?

_____

_____

_____

_____

_____

2. What did you do to discover and realize your potential in the situation?

_____

_____

_____

_____

_____

2. **Vision will be assaulted by criticism.** In the early 2000's, I developed a vision to return to and build up the neighborhood where I was raised as a boy, Westgate in Decatur, Alabama. A low-income area, Westgate was characterized by its project housing and the shopping center featuring a Piggly Wiggly supermarket. Most of the shops and restaurants had moved out, and I desired to bring national brand stores to the old shopping center and build new houses in a rundown old apartment complex. I saw a better life with better amenities for the great people that lived in that neighborhood.

When I did a presentation 15 years ago to the local Rotary Club and to officials at City Hall, they were all on board—but when news of my plan got out to the community, it was instantly attacked and criticized. Some even accused me of simply trying to get rich off the project. I did not let that stop me, though, and while the full project did not come to fruition, we did build a few homes and have since inspired others to invest in the neighborhood.

It was very frustrating that the people complained so much and went against my vision. The city government considered it for two years before we accepted that our plans simply weren't going to come to pass. Today, a subdivision with several homes has been built, but the shopping center is still the same. In all, Westgate is a little better off, but there is still much potential there.

What was the last criticism you received? How did it challenge you?

_____

_____

_____

_____

_____

3. **Vision will develop you.** As I pursue my vision of helping leaders reach their potential by maximizing their core values, it has led me to grow in many areas as well. I have needed to go back to school to get various certificates and training. This vision has placed me at the table with very influential leaders, which has pushed me to improve my communication skills. I have had to increase my financial and business acumen in order to better understand my potential customers. I am driven to get up every day with an expectation to learn and develop.

How have you been developed as you pursued a vision in your life?

_____

_____

_____

_____

_____

A super day for visioncasting

What are the three attributes that make Sunday the ideal day to dream, visualize, and set into motion the visions for your life?

First, it operates in the *law of first*, setting the _____ for the week. Back when I worked for General Motors, I began setting aside time every Sunday afternoon to cast a vision for each upcoming week. I wrote down what projects I wanted to work on and defined the degree of accomplishment for each project and the results I wanted to see. I continue this routine today, and it keeps me in line and on track with my goals. It motivates me to set expectations that are higher than I believe I can accomplish.

I'm the type of person who is always striving beyond my original motivation. As speaker Les Brown is quoted to have said, "Shoot for the moon, and if you miss, you'll still be among the stars." I truly believe that the problem with most people's goals is that they set them just low enough to hit them. Even when I don't hit my goals, I have still accomplished way more than most people can even imagine.

What can you start doing every Sunday to set the expectation for your week?

_____

_____

_____

_____

Second, Sunday is a day of *personal inspiration*, a time we are _____ to go forward. Over 20 years ago, I was inspired to have an hour of self-reflection about my future. I do this every Sunday, usually in the early evening and either in my outdoor gazebo at home or on a motorcycle ride. I ask myself "why," "how," and "when" questions that invite me to dream of my potential accomplishment, entertain ideas, and explore the options presented to me.

Name one specific goal you have for your future.

_____

_____

_____

Now, ask yourself:

1. Why do I want this?

_____

_____

_____

_____

_____

2. How can I best achieve it?

_____

_____

_____

_____

_____

3. When do I want it to come to pass?

_____

_____

_____

_____

_____

Finally, I use Sundays as a weekly opportunity to *establish an intentional tone* for the scope and _____ of the week ahead. I first began this practice when I was in North Carolina working at IBM (International Business Machines Corporation). I wrote down ways I wanted to have a positive attitude for the week, and then I looked at the scope of work as far as who I needed to communicate with and when to provide them the highest level of positive engagement and feedback. I even planned my business attire choices for the week depending on who I was going to meet and where.

I continue to do this today before bedtime every Sunday night. It's a great way to end the day by solidifying my mindset and setting myself at ease about the coming work week.

SCOTT'S STORY

Scott was a caring and selfless individual, but he wasn't exactly known for his cheery disposition. He was often on edge at work at his hardware store, short with his customers, and at odds with the local town selectman. Grumpy and hardheaded, it was not uncommon for him to go on a rant about everything from lawyers and consumerist society to the pitfalls inherent in buying a car or hunting for an apartment. Everything was fair game, and while Scott was a big believer in keeping it real, his diatribes were setting an intentional tone for his days—and not the best one.

Changing his mindset was one of the hardest things he ever did, but over time, Scott succeeded. It started with listening to an audiobook about relationships that helped him to better understand himself and how to better perceive the wants and needs of others. Next, he put his newly learned principles into practice by patching things up with the town selectman and even volunteering to assist him on the restoration project of a historical home. Finally, Scott decreased his focus on the negative attributes of people and the society around him and increased his perception and recognition of the positive.

Everything Scott did to transform himself and his thinking was intentional, and his newfound attitude elevated his already-existing selflessness and care toward others.

Questions for application:

1. Name something that you are consistently negative about. Why does it bring you down?

_____

_____

_____

_____

_____

2. After reading what Scott did, what is one thing you can do intentionally improve your mindset about that and become more positive about it?

_____

_____

_____

_____

_____

3. Which of your already-existing positive aspects will be elevated as a result of changing your attitude? Why?

_____

_____

_____

_____

_____

Some other great things about Sunday are the characteristics uniquely common to the day. For many, it is a day of worship and reflection where our spiritual natures are nourished and activated. By focusing, if only for a few hours, on the _____, our hearts and minds are quieted, positioning us to better hear and ponder new insights or ideas. There was a Sunday in August 2019 when I had the insight to start a new program to talk about leadership. I saw a vision of inviting leaders from different backgrounds to talk live on YouTube about various topics concerning personal growth and leadership.

I was inspired to reach out to several guests, and we started the program called Lead and Achieve with Doc Rock. It currently goes live every second and fourth Thursday evening of each month on the Emmanuel The Connection YouTube channel.

What is something new that you can start doing on Sunday to better focus on the divine?

_____

_____

_____

_____

Sunday is also generally considered to be a day of rest. It's the one day where many people set aside additional time with their families to relax and play. Some use Sundays as an opportunity for a special in-town getaway, to take day trips away from home to see and do new things, or to revisit previous positive experiences. All of these things allow us to _____ our thoughts away from the urgent matters of the rest of the week, enabling us to think more freely and with less distraction.

While taking a ride one Sunday evening on my motorcycle, I was inspired to begin speaking in a different way as a pastor, one that would focus more on personal growth for businessmen and women while still advancing the Kingdom of God. I wanted my sermons to apply to people's everyday lives while breaking away from the traditional approach of an introduction, three points, and a conclusion. I even began bringing people onstage while I taught to supplement what I was sharing. Most of the presentations I now use for corporate America come from those teachings. Since then, my effectiveness as a pastor and as a consultant has been enhanced and deepened.

What can you start doing on Sunday to think more freely and with less distraction?

_____

_____

_____

_____

Because Sunday is situated on the calendar as the starting point of each new week, it is the perfect day for visioncasting—for it is through vision that seven key choices are made that directly impact your life every day.

1. **Vision chooses your future.** Growing up, I had always thought about being a doctor in a hospital. I would read my mom's nursing books, and I took all the science classes I could in high school. One day, while I was contemplating how to get into and pay for medical school, I visited Dr. Kenneth Pitts in Huntsville about a medical career. He was my mother's colleague, so I knew he would be a great person to give me some good advice.

    I told him what I was thinking about doing. "You may very well have the intellect," he replied, "but what is God's vision for you?" He went on to explain that he became a doctor because he felt God had called him to go into that field, and he told me to return to him for help only after I had prayed. I did so—and that was when I was given a vision of leading people to achieve their best.

1. When you were a child, what did you think about being?

    _____

    _____

    _____

    _____

    _____

2. What are you doing now?

    _____

    _____

    _____

    _____

    _____

3. How does that make you feel about your future?

    _____

    _____

    _____

    _____

    _____

2. **Vision chooses your friends.** When I put into motion my vision to be involved with a leadership organization in the northern Alabama region, it led me to becoming friends with the CEO of the organization. Since then, I have met many others who have become close friends and with whom I can share ideas and dreams. Those relationships have benefitted me immensely and have led to the birth of other visions to do good work.

Who is your most beneficial friend? How does that person feed your vision?

_____

_____

_____

_____

_____

3. **Vision chooses your library.** My desire to learn more about how people's minds and emotions operated in concert with one another encouraged me to start reading books about proper mindset and Emotional Intelligence. My library is now full of books on positive thinking and personal and professional discipline, and I read or listen to such content every day, even if it is only for 10 minutes at a time.

Do you read or listen to books for self-improvement? Why or why not?

_____

_____

_____

_____

_____

4. **Vision chooses your priorities.** In 1997, "The Sound and the Fury" boxing match between Evander Holyfield and Mike Tyson for the WBA Heavyweight Championship was the sports event of the year, and several of my friends were getting together to watch it. I really wanted to join them—but because I had a vision for achieving success as a leadership trainer, I had to forego the invitation in order to prepare for a training session. I may have missed the big bite Tyson took from Holyfield's ear that night, but I took a far bigger bite toward meeting my goal and executing my vision by keeping my priorities.

1. What has gone by the wayside in your life so that you can prioritize your vision?

_____

_____

_____

_____

_____

2. Has the result of that choice been a positive one? Why or why not?

_____

_____

_____

_____

_____

5. **Vision chooses your use of time.** There have been many other occasions where my time had to be dedicated to work in order to achieve specific goals. One of those was when I had to spend extra hours as an engineer completing a new project on behalf of Saginaw Steering, a division of my employer, General Motors. The project involved creating an automatic torque machine that served as a wrench that attached a tube to the steering gear. I had a vision to see it come to fruition on deadline and with excellence, and I put in the time necessary to achieve that goal.

How can you better use your time to meet your goals?

_____

_____

_____

_____

_____

6. **Vision chooses your values.** Values are your standards, your principles of behavior. While I was in college, I was at a party where several fellow students were getting drunk, and it looked to me like things were getting out of hand. People were getting rowdy and raucous. I certainly didn't

view myself as being better than anyone else who was there, but my values directed me to leave the party. I didn't want to do anything to undermine my vision of achieving everything I could while in engineering school. I encouraged my friends to be safe before departing, and I have never regretted the decision to honor my values.

Tell the story of a time you chose to honor your values?

_____

_____

_____

_____

_____

7. **Vision chooses your attitude in life.** Countless times, I have made the decision to keep and maintain a positive attitude, especially when under pressure. Ability Plus is an organization subject to an annual state audit regarding the services we provide. In 2021, we were cited in several areas, and the auditor went over all the improvements needed for our organization to be in full compliance. It felt like the world and everyone in it was against me and the company, but I told the auditors that the issues were my responsibility as CEO and that we would address them, knowing it's always best to be proactive rather than reactive.

I had a vision of us going from "good to great," and I challenged everyone using the book of the same name by Jim Collins. Changes were implemented in operations, policies and procedures, and overall work culture. As a result, the staff's mindset was elevated, we dug in, and we worked with a vision of being triumphant. The next audit confirmed a 100-percent improvement in all facets of the company.

What is something you can do at the workplace to go from good to great?

_____

_____

_____

_____

_____

Super Sunday principles to complete your vision

I am always inspired by the stories of others who have achieved greatness. Four stories in particular serve to exemplify my four key principles for completing your vision.

First, you must be willing to *pay the price* regardless of the _____ in front of you. Helen Keller once said, "The only thing worse than being blind is having sight but no vision," and she certainly knew that to be true. Helen was only 19 months old when she lost both her sight and hearing in 1881. Never allowing her physical conditions to limit her, Helen had a vision to achieve greatness in service to others. After attending both specialist and mainstream schools, Helen attended Radcliffe College of Harvard University and became the first deaf and blind person to earn a bachelor's degree. Helen worked for the American Foundation for the Blind from 1924 until 1968, touring the United States and traveling to 35 countries around the globe as an advocate for those with vision loss.

When I was a student at Kettering University (formerly the GMI Engineering & Management Institute), I was voted by my peers to be the president of the Black Unity Congress (BUC). As its leader, I paid the price to fulfill my vision to get others involved in the BUC who were not African American. I wanted the organization to be genuinely supported by the entire student body. Several BUC members had serious reservations about moving in that direction. "If we include whites, are we still about black unity?" "Are they going to take over?" "Are we still going to focus on issues that affect minorities, or are they going to try to address other issues?" My answer was that we were going to bring in others because the issues we addressed were not just about us as African Americans, but they affected everyone.

It took considerable time and effort to convince the BUC that my vision to no longer be a segregated organization was a good idea. Several whites joined, including my good friend, Andrew, who was president of the student body. Under my tenure, we got more involved in the student body, developed a mentorship program with area churches, and sat in on the school's President's Council for the first time. Our funding also quadrupled. It took courage, but we were all willing to pay the price for a better tomorrow.

1. Share how you had to pay the price for what you are achieving today?

_____

_____

_____

_____

_____

2. Was it worth it? Why or why not?

_____

_____

_____

_____

_____

Next, you must be _____ enough to *overcome persecution*. Corrie Ten Boom once said, "I can see further than my eyes can look." It's impossible to imagine the vision she had to develop in order to see beyond her experiences as a survivor of the Holocaust. It couldn't have been easy for Corrie to accept what her Nazi captors had done to her, tormenting her at Ravensbrück and causing the death of her sister, Betsy.

Ten years after her release, Corrie ran into a woman who refused to look her in the eyes. Confused, she asked about the lady, and she was told the woman had been a nurse at a concentration camp. Corrie then recalled taking Betsy to the infirmary to see that very nurse. Betsy was dying, and the woman had been cruel and sharp-tongued. At that moment, Corrie's hatred returned with a vengeance. Her rage so boiled that she knew of only one thing to do—and that was to get a vision to live as a forgiving person.

"Forgive me," she cried out. "Forgive my hatred, oh, Lord. Teach me to love my enemies!"

Suddenly, Corrie felt her anger being displaced with a love she couldn't explain. The next day, Corrie called the hospital where the nurse worked and invited the woman to a meeting where she was speaking. That evening after her talk, Corrie sat down with the nurse and shared how she had come to love God and others despite the atrocities done to her and to her sister. Corrie, overcoming the persecution she had faced was only possible by having a vision to forgive those who had harmed her.[2]

EDWARD'S STORY

A stern, hard-working, old-fashioned husband and father, Edward had lived what he saw as a privileged life, balancing a successful career in finance with his beloved hobbies of golfing and restoring vintage automobiles. He never viewed himself as anyone who would ever have to deal with any sort of trouble and certainly not anything that could be considered persecution.

Then an international corporate takeover of the firm Edward had worked at for over 30 years changed everything. Suddenly, despite his Yale education and vast years of experience, he was forced into early retirement. Age discrimination was never overtly stated, but it was certainly inferred as twenty-somethings took over his position and those of his staff, all of whom were terminated. At first, Edward was hurt and incensed. Lifelong expectations of employer appreciation and loyalty were shattered, and Edward considered legal action.

That's when Edward instead adopted a new vision. What happened to him was unfair, but he knew it would do him no good to dwell on the past or harbor any bitterness against people he didn't even know and couldn't do anything about. Using his pension, and with the assistance of his entrepreneurial daughter, Edward started his own financial firm. Choosing to keep it small, he became a certified financial planner and coach, which gave him more satisfying one-on-one relationships with clients he chose and nurtured who had a variety of investment questions and needs. This resulted in giving Edward more time for his hobbies as well as weekly Friday night dinners with his daughter and granddaughter. Most of all, he overcame the resentment he felt from being discriminated against because of his age.

Questions for application:

1. When have you or someone you know faced persecution that resulted in discrimination? Describe the account.

_____

_____

_____

_____

2. What did you or they do to overcome it and move forward from it?

_____

_____

_____

_____

3. Were the discriminators ever confronted? Why or why not?

_____

_____

_____

_____

_____

Third, completing your vision _____ you to have a *commitment to core values*. Nick Saban is one of the most successful college football coaches in recent history, leading his teams to multiple national titles at Louisiana State University and the University of Alabama. Saban said, "You've got to have a vision of, 'What kind of program do I want to have?' Then you've got to have a plan to implement it. Then you've got to set the example that you want, develop the principles and values that are important, and get people to buy into it."

As told in 2018 by ESPN senior writer Kevin Van Valkenburg in ESPN The Magazine's college football issue, Saban's Alabama Crimson Tide had just defeated the University of Texas 37-21 to win Alabama's first national title since 1992. Here is what quarterback Greg McElroy said Saban told the team in the locker room after that victory. "To you seniors, I just want to thank you for everything you did. Absolutely amazing, everything you put into this program. You didn't choose us as a coaching staff, but you bought in when we got here, and you've been rewarded. We're grateful to you for that contribution." Then he added, "For those of you coming back, that's not the way we play in the second half, and you know that. I'm proud of you, too, but we're going to get that stuff figured out when we get back together in a couple of weeks."

Even at the peak of triumph, Saban remained true to the core values his players had bought into, and he reiterated that vision, which focused on maintaining superior performance on the football field, to his returning athletes—most of whom would respond with more title-winning performances in the future.

There was a time when a company I led was riding high. It was part of our core values to care for our staff at all of our locations, and we definitely had a dedicated team of workers who believed in our mission and were willing to sacrifice so we could be our best. We received some extra funding that could have been used for other programs, but I decided instead to give it to every person in the company in the form of bonuses to assist in their everyday lives. I felt that if we helped them individually to maximize who they were, then collectively we would maximize who *we* were. People were encouraged as we stayed true to our core values. It showed them that they mattered to us and that we valued their service.

Do you have a set of core values? If so, list and define them. If not, what one core value would you name and define as being foundational to your life?

_____

_____

_____

_____

_____

Finally, you must *develop patience* to _____ your vision. The late, great leadership expert and minister Dr. Myles Munroe once said, "Vision is eternity positioned in time." He knew this truth from an early age. When he was 14, Munroe learned that a trusted teacher from the United Kingdom had referred to him as a "black monkey" and said that "black people cannot learn sophisticated things." Humiliated and upset, Munroe told his mother about the insults. In response, she got out her Bible and instructed him to read Ephesians 3:20, which said God could help him do "exceedingly abundantly above all that we ask or think."

That message changed Munroe's mindset as he understood that power did not reside in his teacher's racist words but rested within. Patiently, Munroe pursued his education, graduated at the top of his class, and went on to college to obtain no less than three bachelor's degrees, a master's degree, and five doctorates. As he did, he became a speaker whose words had an eternal impact on the lives of others. What became of the teacher who insulted him? Munroe eventually met him in person at a leadership conference—and the teacher, who asked Munroe to autograph two books Munroe had written, apologized for way he had viewed Munroe as a student. Munroe replied, "Don't you ever again underestimate a human," and they embraced.[3]

I was born to a 15-year-old mother who taught me that I could achieve anything I put my mind to as long as I had the patience to pursue it. When I turned 16, I drove around my mom's little wrecked Toyota while my peers were driving their own new or used cars that were in much better shape than mine. I wanted us to have a different car, among other things, yet I knew that if I worked hard in school and made good grades, I could produce something great for us in the future.

I patiently studied with expectation and anticipation that there would come a day when I could afford to have and do things that were not available to me then. I developed a mindset of delayed gratification, a principle that creates time to build money, talent, or resources in order to obtain something. That patience has paid off with a successful career that has generated wealth and resources for me and my family.

KELLY'S STORY

Kelly was never one for patience. Not good at dealing with her emotions or showing vulnerability, Kelly put forth a frank demeanor and could be manipulative and vindictive when required. Unfortunately, this often set her at odds with her family, particularly her grown daughter, and left her with few friends outside of her limited social circles.

After her divorce was finalized, Kelly came up with a rather unusual and unlikely vision: move to Europe and teach history. History was always her love, and she had majored in it in college. "I've never done anything," she reflected to her daughter in a rare moment of openness one night over dinner. "But I'm all alone, and I don't know what to do."

Moved by her mother's plight (in part because she was more like her mother than she'd ever care to admit), Kelly's daughter decided to help. Together, they researched teaching opportunities and planned the international move from the northeastern States. In the process, the pair butted heads more than once, but Kelly was determined to change—and she discovered patience was the virtue she was most lacking. She went to work on herself, including therapy, and began responding differently to circumstances and starting to heal from past hurts.

In all, it took a year in the life of Kelly, but she and her daughter made her vision a reality and they grew closer as a result. Today, Kelly is a humanities professor at The American University of Paris teaching history with the American Revolution as a specialty, and she looks forward to regular summer visits from her daughter.

Questions for application:

1. What are the two triggers that cause you to lose patience the most?

   _____

   _____

2. How have those triggers and your impatience undermined your vision for your life?

   _____

   _____

   _____

   _____

   _____

3. What can you do in the next year to address those triggers and move toward inner healing?

_____

_____

_____

_____

_____

Starting each week with renewed vision acts as a preview of things to come, setting the stage for success and allowing you to go into your Monday with momentum. Why?

Vision brings positive change. Sure, he was just a blacksmith, but Will Turner was also an artisan at creating beautiful swords, and he developed a vision to become expert at wielding them. As he dueled against the renegade buccaneer, Captain Jack Sparrow, inside the smithy where his swords were displayed, Will boasted, "I practice three hours a day so that when I meet a pirate, I can kill him!"

If you've seen the motion picture *Pirates of the Caribbean: The Curse of the Black Pearl*, you'll remember that later, at the opportune moment, Will's training paid off as he teamed with Jack to fight off the Pearl's crew, end the curse, and rescue the governor's fair daughter.

Developing and _____ your vision will have a similarly life-changing impact on yourself and those around you. When it comes to vision, I've learned that 10 percent of people are Pioneers, meaning they are those who desire to put in the work and take the risks necessary to fulfill their vision. They are on the cutting edge in their field and see what has not yet been produced. The next group are Settlers and account for 70 percent of individuals. They are those who just settle for the status quo, going with the flow and preferring the norm when it comes to what they see and experience. They are capable of developing and rehearsing their vision, but they choose not to.

Finally, the remaining 20 percent of people are Antagonistic. They are those who are negative about visioncasting and tend to see all of the potholes in the road instead of the road itself. They don't put in the work to create a vision because they don't even see the vision in the first place. About 15 years ago, my church had a vision to move to a new location. A few of our people (Pioneers) were very excited and willing to do whatever was necessary to make the move a success. Most (Settlers) were fine with moving and had no complaints, but they were not going to go out of their way to help make it happen. Then there was the last group (Antagonists) who loved to find the speck in the milk. They were negative about most everything having to do with the move.

In a business setting, Settlers rely on others to build the company and achieve its vision. They don't rely on themselves. They look to leadership to do it all. They do their jobs, go home, and come in the next morning to do their job again. Sometimes the culture of a company pushes that mindset to the forefront because it doesn't get people involved in change. As leaders, then, knowing the Pioneers are on board, we focus on the Settlers. Our management and teaching efforts target them with the hope that some might come over and join the 10 percent.

Knowing that there will be confrontation with the Antagonists, leaders should treat them well, but not allow them to undermine the vision. "Okay," we tell them, "you have your opinion. You see a different way, and that's fine." Yet leaders are to listen to the 20 percent and not alienate them. While they may come across as negative and critical, there could still be legitimacy in some of the things they say. We can learn from them to make the process better.

1. Are you a Pioneer, Settler, or Antagonist? Why?

_____

_____

_____

_____

2. Who do you struggle with the most: Pioneers, Settlers, or Antagonists? Why?

_____

_____

_____

_____

Vision fosters innovation and creativity, empowering you beyond your existing assets. Jupiter is a massive planet buffeted by immense storms. Scientists speculate these gigantic tempests, swirling with 400 mile-per-hour winds, have been raging unabated for hundreds of years. But it wasn't until recently that they learned the source of Jupiter's ultra-potent storms. The Galileo space probe revealed that they're generated not by sunlight, as are storms on Earth, but by the planet itself. Jupiter's storms actually churn 10,000 miles into the planet and are powered by its sizzling hot core.

Everything viewed on the surface of Jupiter starts at the very heart of the planet—and anything new and inventive in your life that's going to rise to the surface begins with the vision churning within you at your core, providing you the ability to see what others cannot.

When I was a young engineer working for Delphi, a division of General Motors, a vision was brewing within me to make a specific process (torquing a nut onto a tube) more efficient and reliable. It had been done the same way for years using a manual torque wrench gauge. The gauge was employed at the end of a process that had five stations. That meant that by the time the tube got to the inspection station, there was a chance that as many as five of the nuts were not properly torqued. My vision would electronically check each individual torque station and stop the line when there was an error. This required new electronic torque guns (the tools that tighten the nuts) as well as the updated process arrangement.

We called a team meeting to talk about the current process and how it functioned. I then shared how I saw the new process working. Instead of having a person on the end of the line that checked all the parts after they were torqued, I proposed that each person would have a gun to check the particular nut they were working on at their station. Whenever a bad torque happened, everybody had to be patient and wait for that person to retorque it. We also had to ensure that, whenever a bad part was detected, there was a person in charge of getting the replacement part and putting it in the proper bin. It took three months from start to finish, but we implemented my vision, and it increased both productivity and quality.

Why didn't others see what I did? Most people kept their head down, concerned only about the process instead of saying, "This is good, but how can it be better?"

I always say, "Good, better, best. Never let it rest until your good is better and your better is best." A good thing can be a bad thing if it's not the best thing, yet most people _____ for good.

1. Describe one area professionally where you know you are settling for good?

_____

_____

_____

_____

_____

2. What two things can you do right now to begin moving toward better to arrive at best?

_____

_____

_____

_____

_____

Vision causes simplicity. Clergyman Robert Fulghum became famous because of his essay, "All I Really Need to Know I Learned in Kindergarten." He suggested that the simple rules learned in kindergarten will do for life. Share everything. Play fair. Don't hit people. Put things back where you found them. Clean up your own mess. Flush.

Simplicity eliminates _____, bringing clarity of purpose and providing direction. There was a process change that I felt would make things work much smoother with our internal structure at Ability Plus. The vision was to streamline the roles of our Qualified Intellectual Disabled Professional (QIDP) staff into two different categories: office-specific and field-specific. As it was, our QIDP's were responsible for all the paperwork, including the processing forms required by the state, along with any issues that happened in the field, in the house, or with our clients. With the new process, half of them would be responsible for office work and the other half for field duties. That would allow each QIDP to operate within their strengths and work together to get the job done, bringing greater value to the entire team. The new vision's strength was how it brought a sense of order and created simplicity.

SEAN'S STORY

To describe Sean as eccentric would be an understatement. A sweet young man who meant well, Sean could also be irrational and, at times, a nuisance to himself and others. His unpredictable personality was largely informed by his mother, an invisible but seemingly overbearing presence in his adult life, and his awkwardness with personal relationships. Vocationally, Sean flitted from one job to another, and while he was innovative in his own ways, he could never stay with one thing very long before moving on to the next.

That's when Sean got a vision for filmmaking. Not only did it seem an obvious release for his restless creativity, but it also allowed him to leverage some of the very eccentricities that often undermined his other ventures. That vision also forced him to narrow and simplify his thinking. This was necessary to help him strategically manage his project schedule, as well as the other technicians and performers involved. To Sean's amazement, he discovered how simplicity actually quieted his mind, even as it made him more focused and productive.

When his first short film was released, it was met with mostly positive reviews for the stark, film noir cinematography and inventive use of interpretive dance—and it resulted in a contract from a large studio for a full-length feature. Sean finally found professional clarity of purpose that is now having a positive influence on his personal life.

Questions for application:

1. When was the last time simplification helped you through a dilemma?

    _____

    _____

    _____

    _____

    _____

2. Looking at your own personality traits, which one can be best leveraged for your current vision? How?

    _____

    _____

    _____

    _____

    _____

3. If you could do anything you wanted, what would it be?

    _____

    _____

    _____

    _____

    _____

Violins made by masters like Antonio Stradivari produce an incomparably beautiful sound and sell for millions to investors. But excellent violins are not like works of art, to be hung on a wall or displayed under glass. They'll lose their tone if not played regularly, and they actually increase in value the more they're used. That's why the Stradivari Society exists. It puts those first-rate violins into the hands of great violin virtuosos to ensure the instruments are preserved, cared for, and played. The musicians are even required to give the violin owners two command performances each year.

You possess a prized possession more valuable than any worldly investment: your attitude. As you change your mindset, you will become a virtuoso at whatever you do—and there's no better day than Monday to establish your attitude for the week.

Super Sunday—Vision **Fill-in-the-Blank Answer Key:**

starts	sequence	complete
see	divine	rehearsing
are	redirect	settle
purpose	obstacles	complication
expectation	strong	
compelled	requires	

[2]

MARVELOUS MONDAY
Attitude

Both the hummingbird and the vulture fly over our nation's deserts. All vultures see is rotting meat because that is what they are looking for. They thrive on that diet. But hummingbirds ignore the smelly flesh of dead animals. Instead, they look for the colorful blossoms of desert plants. They fill themselves with freshness and life. Vultures live on what was. They feed on the past. Hummingbirds live on what is. They seek new life from the present.

That insightful story, as told by writer Steve Goodier in Reader's Digest's Quote Magazine, illustrates a tremendous truth about attitude. We feed upon and become what we see—not with our eyes, but with our _____. There is nothing as powerful as your mindset, and as I often say, "You are today what you thought yesterday, and you will be tomorrow what you are thinking today."

Is your general mindset focused most often on the past or on the present? Why?

_____

_____

_____

_____

_____

Mondays become marvelous when we start each workweek with the right mindset, and mindset begins and ends with _____. Prior to this book, I wrote and published *God-A-Tude*, which focuses on developing an attitude that brings success to life, and I mentioned how surprised I was that many people are simply not aware of how their attitude plays such a major part in their success. Yet more opportunities have been lost, withheld, or forfeited because of attitude than from any other cause.

Yet attitude is our way of thinking. It is the mindset, or _____ conditioning, that determines our interpretation of, and response to, our environments. Your attitude dictates how you react to the present, and it determines the quality of your future. It creates your world and designs your destiny. You are your attitude, and your attitude is you. If you do not control your attitude, it will control you.

Does your attitude currently inform how you react to the present in a positive way or a negative one? Why?

_____

_____

_____

_____

_____

Having a "champion" mindset

Monday is marvelous because it possesses four distinct attributes that allow you to win!

1. **Monday positions you to be humble.** The first day of the workweek can appear awfully daunting, even after you've done everything you can on Sunday to ready yourself for the week ahead. Therefore, you can respond in one of two ways. You can pridefully rush forward into it, or you can humbly step back a moment, assess it, and then move onward in calm confidence. Humility is both a bedrock trait and a powerful _____ in your "champion" mindset. The definition of "humble" is telling: "showing a modest estimate of one's own importance." Isn't that remarkable?

   The way up is down. You have to get down before you can go up!

   From the time I was 17 until my mid-thirties, I felt like I was better than other people. I knew I had been gifted to achieve, and in those 18 years I had experienced success. There I was, this guy from government housing who was traveling around the world teaching leadership principles for life. I had become a little full of myself, lacking in proper humility. Then, in 2008, the economy tanked, and organizations began to struggle. My support system started to crumble. Many who had been contributing to my travel expenses stopped supporting me. Organizations were not asking me to come as frequently as they once did. Just like that, I came back to earth, and as I examined what was going on, I realized I had become arrogant in my outlook.

   That caused me to take a long look at *myself*. Today, I refer to this introspection as a checkup from the neck up and a look around from the shoulders down. I asked, "Am I doing what I am doing for fame or to impress people, or am I doing it to help people?" It was a great question. I came to the conclusion that I wanted to help others—but to do that, I had to remove all of the self-serving perks that came from people saying I'd done a good job or patting me on the back. Receiving accolades is fine as long as you keep it in proper _____.

In all, it took several months for me to change my attitude so that I wasn't going in thinking people needed to treat me as some prima donna, but as a servant. "Can I help them?" "Are they receptive?" "Can I maximize their potential?" It had to stop being about me, and it had to start being about them.

When was the last time you gave yourself "a checkup from the neck up and a look around from the shoulders down?" Share the story and the outcome.

_____

_____

_____

_____

_____

Walking in a position of humility requires you to accept that you have _____. Everyone does, but many will not acknowledge them, which in the end, generally leads to times of struggle. I often tell others that they will grow when they exalt their strengths and work on their weaknesses. In my case, my weaknesses were arrogance and impatience. The strengths I exalted were that I engaged people, made them feel good, and could show individuals and organizations a vision so they could proceed.

To be humble, you must also be open to correction and the opportunity to learn from others who are ahead of you. _____ and _____ are the best ways to do this. Working with a mentor is crucial, and coaching takes that another step, allowing you to systematically put into practice what you learn with your mentor. Simply put, when you take the time and dedicate the money to invest in yourself, it is always going to pay dividends greater than you can anticipate.

1. List three of your weaknesses?

_____

_____

_____

2. List three of your strengths?

_____

_____

_____

3. Describe how you can best leverage your strengths to either offset or minimize your weaknesses.

_____

_____

_____

_____

_____

2. **Monday encourages you to have self-control.** Monday is the one day of the week when you don't want things to get _____ from you. Otherwise, you can't help but feel like you're always having to play catch up. So, while there will be situations that you cannot control, you can control yourself—what you think, how you operate, and the way you respond to the circumstances that come your way. To be someone who exhibits an ability to control your emotions and moderate your words and actions, you cannot allow a flash of negative emotions to produce negative results.

    Self-control is all about holding it together when your world seems to be falling apart.

    I remember a time as a chief operating officer when my chief executive officer treated me like I was a nobody without any respect. He made demands on my time without asking me if I had the time available. It was always his way or no way. At one point, I felt like I was an angry kid back in the projects, and I wanted to knock him out!

    Yet I knew that my future had promise, and I told myself that it was not worth it to respond that way. I also decided that my philosophy of being a servant leader would eventually rise to the top and show others who I really was. I exercised self-control by telling myself that the company and the people who worked for me were more important than my desire to prove a point or do something that I would regret.

CHAD'S STORY

Chad possessed a variety of strengths that informed his character: ceaselessly helpful and caring toward others, Chad was also very intellectual and passionate about writing. However, abandonment issues from being raised in a home broken by divorce and from being bullied in high school made him insecure and impetuous as an adult, especially in his relationships with the opposite sex. He struggled with long-term commitment that sometimes spilled over to his profession. He often felt like he was playing catch up, directionless and unable to control himself or his responses to his circumstances in times when his world seemed like it was unraveling.

However, Chad's greatest strength, his resilience, helped him to use his experiences to gradually address his weaknesses and bring balance and cohesion to his life. Over time, he reconciled with and married the girl he'd loved since middle school. Professional stability followed, and his self-control blossomed and solidified.

His improved mindset determined his attitude and, ultimately, the altitude of his life. Chad developed a vision of where he was going and what he wanted to be as a man and looked ahead at his desired future, learning to accept temporary pain to get to long-term joy. As a result, he felt like a comet blazing across a raven-colored sky! Communicating one of his greatest lessons learned, Chad said, "It's okay to let yourself be happy because you never know how fleeting that happiness might be."

Questions for application:

1. How have the weaknesses and strengths you listed earlier impacted your self-control?

_____

_____

_____

_____

_____

2. Chad's resilience lifted him to new heights. Tell the story of a time you were resilient.

_____

_____

_____

_____

_____

3. Write, as a quotation, one of your greatest lessons learned.

_____

_____

_____

_____

_____

3. **Monday inspires you to have a willingness to learn.** On Monday, there is almost always something new or unexpected that beckons or forces you to acquire _____ you didn't have before or to recall something you previously learned and apply it. To gather ideas from a variety of sources, accurately evaluate the situation, and combine good ideas with the details of the circumstance in order to make changes in your behavior, personally or organizationally, is an essential component of maintaining a "champion" mindset.

You must use information to address your situation.

I was originally educated as an engineer: learning formulas, equations, and science in general. Then I was given the opportunity to learn, as a coach and consultant, how to help people reach their dreams and goals in life. Executive and leadership coaching required a new set of skills to move on to what I needed to know to succeed.

I embraced the new material as a student of change and a pupil of understanding. During my training program, I went through actual scenarios of how to talk to people and the questions to ask them as a coach. I did role playing. I read books on becoming a better listener. After an intense three months of learning, I was released to do some executive coaching, in part because of my previous background of being a church pastor and administrator. I continued training once a week for another year before I was fully let go. It was a full year from the time I began my training before I launched the Vision Excellence Company.

You will inspire yourself to learn when you see a benefit that is greater than the sacrifice of the learning process. When I first started training, I saw what other coaches and consultants were doing for organizations, and I thought becoming a coach and consultant would benefit me and the companies that hired me. Learning is the necessary _____ to plant in order to gain the greater harvest you are looking for in your life. Learners are achievers!

Just as I, the engineer, learned to be a coach and consultant, what new thing would you like to learn? Why?

_____

_____

_____

_____

4. **Monday compels you to have a drive for more.** When you've done the vision casting and preparation I recommend on Sunday, you can't help but go into Monday excited and optimistic, and that breeds M.O.R.E. (Multiple Opportunities Regardless of Everything against you). In every aspect of your life and career, there are greater heights to be experienced, greater accomplishments to achieve, greater impact to be had, greater knowledge to be obtained, greater wisdom to be acquired, greater good to be done—and, yes, more customers to acquire, more markets to penetrate, more employees to hire, more revenue to realize, and more influence to extend.

You are to go more, do more, and be more than you ever thought before!

"I want more!" That was what I told myself in 2018 when things were going well with Vision Excellence Company. I appreciated the opportunities to teach leadership in non-profit settings, but I knew I had more to give to for-profit companies and organizations. I had loved, and still love, teaching church leaders, but I wanted to expand. That required more study and additional branding to broaden my influence.

That's when I created "Doc Rock." The brand is more than just a simple play on my credentials and my name. "Doc Rock" literally communicates expertise and stability, and it suggests engagement, servanthood, and leadership. That new brand, and the services I provide through it, such as my twice-weekly video sessions via YouTube, have led me to go into many areas of motivational speaking and all types of leadership and business trainings that were previously unavailable to me.

To push yourself for more, you must ask yourself, "Is where I am now *all* that I want to do?"

JAMES' STORY

James found himself asking that very question after an injury forced him to reevaluate his desire to have a career as an athlete. A college scholarship offer was his if he wanted it, but he also knew further damage to the same area of his body could result in him being permanently disabled.

It was tough. James had already overcome so much from his troubled teen years of promiscuity, arrogance, and a toxic relationship with his dysfunctional parents. He'd worked hard to become a better version of himself, becoming kinder, selfless, and caring, and that had compelled him to want more for his life. Now, this latest challenge meant that James may have to redefine how he would achieve the "more" that he desired.

With the help and support of his fiancé, James did just that—giving up his dream of being a professional athlete to pursue another equally difficult and potentially elusive goal: acting. He sacrificed whatever he could, without endangering his fledging marriage, to take classes and get auditions. Ultimately, James was given a role in a television series, and his career as an actor grew along with his family. Vocationally and personally, James became more than he ever thought he could by continuing to face adversity with a tenacious mindset and a positive attitude. Instead of wondering what he had to do or who he was supposed to be, James discovered that he didn't want to be anything other than himself.

Questions for application:

1. What is the greatest setback you've faced professionally?

    _____

    _____

    _____

    _____

    _____

2. How did you respond to that setback, and how did it affect your career?

    _____

    _____

    _____

    _____

    _____

3. Assess how that incident impacted your desire for "more" in your life.

    _____

    _____

    _____

    _____

    _____

Monday is also marvelous because of its three identifying characteristics that build and support your "champion" mindset.

1. **Monday is a day that promotes work ethic.** If there is ever a "nose to the grindstone" day in the week, it is Monday. You want to dig in and get things off to a productive start. This requires constantly looking for ways to do things more effectively and efficiently. Such diligence is often what propels already-successful people to start their own businesses and strive for even more greatness.

    Work _____ is that something extra that gets you out of bed when others are still hitting the snooze button.

In 1992, I was fresh out of college and working for IBM as a young engineer. Another team member and I were given a project that required more time than usual to complete. It involved taking an existing printed circuit board and repurposing it for a better use. This necessitated getting to the office early for several weeks and included many late evenings staying at work and testing the new process. Our strong shared work ethic caused us to have great success with the project, and it paid off (literally) with both of us receiving a nice monetary award.

To create and maintain your work ethic, you must major on what is important and set proper priorities. Work ethic is all about performing at the highest level to achieve the highest result!

1. How would you describe your work ethic? Answer honestly.

_____

_____

_____

_____

_____

2. What can you change to improve your work ethic?

_____

_____

_____

_____

_____

2. **Monday is a day that requires the courage of a lion.** Isn't it uncanny how often the adage of Murphy's Law—anything that can go wrong will go wrong—comes to pass on a Monday? There's no telling why this is, but I know I've faced my share of difficulties at the start of the workweek. These trials have usually extended themselves into the rest of the week, and they have necessitated courage to see them through. Courage is the choice and willingness to _____ uncertainty, intimidation, danger, and even agony. Physical courage can manifest itself as a result of enduring pain and hardship. Moral courage can show itself in the face of opposition, shame, scandal, discouragement, or personal loss.

Courage is being scared to death but going forward anyway.

When I was asked to become the CEO of Ability Plus years ago, I could have been quite cowardly. The company was in a very bad financial position. The culture within the organization was toxic at best, and there was no strategic plan or outlook for the near future. I knew I had the leadership skills within me to build a team that could turn it around—but the fear that I might fail required me to summon courage like I never had before. Of course, I could have simply walked away and went somewhere else, but I saw a bright future for the organization beyond what my eyes were seeing and my emotions were feeling.

So, with knees shaking and heart pounding, I went before the entire company employee team and said, "We can do it! We can be one of the best in the industry!" I attacked my fear with courage and exhorted the other leadership and staff at Ability Plus to do the same. In less than a year, the company was on sure footing and would ultimately set the standard for serving people with intellectual disabilities.

To courageously confront whatever obstacles come against you on Monday, or any day, develop a mindset that you will either win or learn, but you cannot lose! Do not be afraid of failure. In fact, see failure as what it is: a part of the winning equation.

SOPHIA'S STORY

When she started high school, Sophia was largely a self-centered party girl and wannabe Queen Bee who was more interested in popularity and boys than anything else. That came mostly from her broken relationship with her mother and father, parents who never wanted a child, tried to buy her love with money, and moved across country when she was only fifteen, leaving her alone in their home to fend for herself with nothing more than a high credit card limit. However, by the time she graduated, Sophia had taken lessons learned from some challenging relationship experiences to mature and change into a kind-hearted, selfless, independent young woman, developing a dogged tenaciousness along the way.

Part of that determination manifested itself in her desire to become the type of mother she'd never had herself. Against all odds, Sophia became a foster mother to a baby girl. But when that child was adopted months later, the loss devastated Sophia. She wondered if she would ever be a mom.

That's when Brooke came into her life. A troubled teen who had bounced from one foster home to the next, Brooke had a lot of qualities Sophia recognized from her own adolescence. Though she was only a decade older than Brooke, Sophia believed she could make a difference in the girl's life. Once more, Sophia bucked the odds and was allowed to become Brooke's foster mother. It took a tireless will and plenty of courage, but Sophia helped Brooke change her behavior and her outlook on life—and by the time Brooke left Sophia's home after her high school graduation, Sophia received word that there was a newborn she could adopt, a girl named Peyton.

Sophia became the mother she always hoped to be, and then some. Today, she is married and has given birth to two more children, Lucas and Haley. About her attitude, Sophia said, "There's a day when you realize that you're not just a survivor, you're a warrior. You're tougher than anything life throws your way."

Questions for application:

1. For Sophia, it was abandonment. What is the main obstacle you've had to overcome to become who you are today?

_____

_____

_____

_____

_____

2. How did you use courage to buck the odds against you caused by that obstacle?

_____

_____

_____

_____

_____

3. How has failure proven to be part of the winning equation in your life?

_____

_____

_____

_____

_____

3. **Monday is a day that necessitates synergy.** On a day where unexpected challenges or stress can sometimes spur argument and division, the ability to have synergy is vital. I love the definition of synergy. Read it carefully. It is "an interaction or cooperation giving rise to a whole that is greater than the simple sum of its parts." Wow! The term "synergy" comes from the Greek word *synergia* and means "working together."

Over the years, I've discovered that most people _____ in life—either with others at their own level, or, if they are seeking rapid growth, with those who are far more advanced than them. Yet a better approach is to avoid competition and, instead, collaborate with others who are ahead of you.

Likewise, if you want to do incredible work, partner with people who are more talented than you. One of the richest Americans of all time, industrialist and philanthropist Andrew Carnegie, said that teamwork appeared most effective when each individual helped others to succeed. The synergy of that team increased as each person contributed. The different skills of each team member also improved, which increased the efficiency of the team and developed its unity.

In everything you do, there should be collaborative and synergistic elements in play.

One of the best trainings I ever did was when my friend, Jeff Bright, and I collaborated on a presentation about Emotional Intelligence. Our synergy was amazing. We are very different in many ways, but those differences allowed us to pull on each other from all directions and to communicate to our audience in a much broader and deeper way. He was better than me in some areas; I was better than him in others. But together we taught about Emotional Intelligence in a way that was truly "greater than the simple sum of its parts." We received many positive comments on the effectiveness of our training.

In order to achieve synergy when divisive challenges arise, you must be open to new ideas and new ways of doing things. You should also be humble enough to accept that someone may have a better process than you that will make *you* better as you work together. Don't compete. Collaborate!

BETHANY'S STORY

An intelligent and funny overachiever, Bethany always liked to help people when they needed it, and she believed there was good in everyone. Therefore, the ability to collaborate came easily to Bethany, but she had to be careful. Naturally protective toward herself and others, Bethany treasured honesty and abhorred betrayal. So, collaboration came with the risk that Bethany could be taken advantage of and even hurt by those in whom she placed her trust.

Knowing that she had to face that fear head-on, Bethany utilized her emotional intelligence, in combination with her automatic inclination toward kindness, to counter her apprehensions with a fierce determination to place confidence in, and depend on, the people she partnered with. To entrust herself and her heart to others wasn't always easy, but Bethany wouldn't be deterred.

Two incredible collaborations, both with longtime friends, came out of her transformed attitude: a music recording company that survived a hostile takeover attempt, and the reopening of a beloved café in her hometown. "We spend so much time wanting, pursuing, wishing," Bethany said of herself and her mindset on life. "But ambition is good. Chasing things with integrity is good. Dreaming."

Questions for application:

1. As you think about collaborating with others, what fear or perceived limitation comes to mind?

\
\
\
\
\

2. Using Bethany's mindset change as inspiration, what can you do to alter your attitude and overcome?

\
\
\
\
\

3. What is the dream you'd like to chase with integrity? How might collaboration make that dream a reality?

\
\
\
\
\

Monday mental strength

The Chicago Tribune once told of an interesting study where one group of volunteers was given a report stating that the "Monday blues" are real. The second was provided an article refuting its existence. A final group was given nothing at all. Guess what happened? The first group was most likely to rate Monday as the worst day of the week.[4]

If you firmly believe that Monday is always going to be a difficult day, odds are good it will be, but only because your attitude is dictating your outlook. A "champion" mindset requires you to be mentally strong—and your Monday will always be marvelous when you define the day by living out these 10 principles of mentally strong people.

Fight through hurt and pain

You always have two choices when things begin to get tough: you can either overcome an obstacle and _____ in the process, or you can let it beat you. If you quit when things get difficult, it'll be that much easier to quit the next time. On the other hand, if you force yourself to push through a challenge, your mental strength increases.

Years ago, while I was serving as a senior leader in church ministry, a person who was dear to the organization decided to leave. This particular individual had several key roles of responsibility, was close to my family, and was someone I trusted. If I could have carved out an executive assistant position for her, I would've done it 100 times over. I asked her to stay, but I realized it was selfish to want something for me when the departure would be better for her. I had to process that there would be pain, hurt, and disappointment as we grew and moved forward. In the end, the move was best for her, and going through it made me stronger as a leader.

What can you change about your attitude to force yourself to push through challenges?

_____

_____

_____

_____

_____

Be patient and delay gratification

The delay of gratification and patience are essential to success and mental strength. I once wanted everything right now—but that all changed when I had to wait for opportunities to be a keynote speaker and facilitator of seminars at major company events. I had the work ethic and the talent to do it immediately, and I wanted to experience the feeling of being valued as I walked out onto the big stage. I could see the lights and hear my name being announced. The atmosphere of success screamed at me, but I had to train my mind to endure every aspect of the hard work, critique, challenges, and pain necessary to see that manifested.

During this time of delayed gratification, I learned that my _____ was getting in the way. I had to stop making it about me and instead become humble and selfless, making it about others. It required a mindset shift where, instead of seeing what being a keynote speaker and facilitator would do for me and my success, I needed to focus on the value I would add to those I would serve. Going through that process gave me the right perspective and attitude when that level of success finally arrived.

What can you change about your attitude to improve your ability to delay gratification?

_____

_____

_____

_____

_____

Fail, make mistakes, and try again—without flinching

When I was a young church pastor, we had a vibrant, growing ministry. But there came a time when the wheels fell off after I changed how I shared my sermons and presented my ministry to target a broader audience. We lost our members, revenue, and building. I fully believed in what I was doing, but I felt like a failure at first. I was embarrassed, too, and it was as if I had slipped into a deep, dark hole with no help or light in sight.

My mind told me to stop, but my heart said to go forward and keep moving ahead despite negative comments or concerns. I couldn't predicate my feelings and choices on a bunch of other people, and I began to instead view my perceived failure as a part of success. I got to the point where I didn't care what people thought. I only cared about what I was called to do. I didn't flinch, and over time, the ministry recovered, and its impact expanded.

What can you change about your attitude to better see failure as a small, but necessary, step in the process of reaching your goals?

_____

_____

_____

_____

_____

Keep your emotions and feelings in check

Negative emotions challenge your mental strength. While it's impossible not to feel your emotions, it is completely within your power to _____ them effectively and to keep yourself in control of them. A bad mood can make you lash out or stray from your chosen direction just as easily as a good mood can make you overconfident and impulsive. There was a time that I got very angry when a person falsely accused me of a wrongdoing. That individual sent targeted emails to specific people that painted me in a bad light. I wanted to lash out, but I knew that was not the right thing to do. I kept my emotions in check, maintained the right perspective, and it worked out for my good. The truth came out, I was exonerated, and the company came out in a favorable light.

What can you change about your attitude to control your emotions and feelings?

_____

_____

_____

_____

_____

Make the calls you're afraid to make

Sometimes you have to do things you don't want to do because you know they're for the best. It's easy to let such challenges paralyze you, but mentally strong people know that, in these moments, the best thing they can do is to get started right away. Every moment spent dreading the task subtracts time and energy from actually getting it done.

At Ability Plus, there was a time when I had to make a call to keep or drop a critical service at the company. There was no doubt that the service was needed in the community, but we simply did not have the proper resources and company buy-in to achieve excellence and success with that service. After much internal debate, I cancelled the service. Thankfully, we were able to find assistance to help relocate the service with another organization.

HILARIE'S STORY

"Others never stay." From her upbringing to her relationships, a pervading sense of abandonment was Hilarie's mantra in life. That she became a fiercely independent woman with a guarded heart was no surprise to the few individuals Hilarie let into her life well enough to say they truly knew her.

So, it was no wonder Hilarie felt alone and on her own when she was faced with a career choice that would either make or break her. She could play it safe and settle for where she was and what she was doing, or she could break out of her comfort zone, take on the uncertainty, and expose herself to potential epic failure. Hilarie didn't want to do it, but she was convinced the new job opportunity could benefit her professionally and certainly *would* be the best thing for her personally.

Drawing on the mental strength she'd accumulated through her hardships, Hilarie didn't wait. She accepted the position, made the move, and threw herself into her new life with everything she had. At times, fear threatened to freeze her in her tracks, but she determinedly trudged forward.

What happened? Hilarie not only succeeded in her career, but the relocation led to her introduction to Sawyer, the person who would eventually shatter her mantra and become her best friend and partner for life.

Questions for application:

1. In the past year, what task have you dreaded so much that it drained your time and energy?

_____

_____

_____

_____

_____

2. How have you responded to that challenge?

_____

_____

_____

_____

_____

3. What life mantra do you have to address to face your fears and have a better attitude?

_____

_____

_____

_____

_____

Trust your gut

There's a fine line between doing this well and being impulsive. Trusting your gut is a matter of looking at a decision from every possible _____. Then, when the facts don't present a clear alternative, believe in your ability to make the right decision.

I had to follow my gut when I was presented with a plan for restructuring at Ability Plus. We streamlined the roles of our Qualified Intellectual Disabled Professional (QIDP) staff into two different categories: office-specific and field-specific. It had never been done that way before, and it was unnerving for some. Yet I'm so glad I went with my gut and made half of them responsible for office work and the other half for field duties. We may not have made it through the COVID-19 pandemic intact, when it hit in early 2020, had we not had the new structure.

What can you change about your attitude to believe more in your ability to make the right decision?

_____

_____

_____

_____

_____

Lead when no one else follows

It's not hard to set a direction and to believe in yourself when you have support, but the true test of mental strength is how well you maintain your resolve when nobody else believes in what you are doing. Stay the course as you try to win people over to your way of thinking. After all, a true vision is worth pursuing, even when you have to go it alone.

When I first started my quest to do paid leadership training seminars and events, there were many people who did not believe I would succeed. It may have seemed they were right when some of my early seminars went largely unattended except for the few individuals I had hired to work the event. But I just kept preparing material, leading, and believing until people started to show up. When no one was there, I still taught the seminar. It was great practice, and it solidified the material in my mind.

What can you change about your attitude to maintain your resolve when nobody else believes in what you are doing?

_____

_____

_____

_____

_____

Focus on the details even when it makes your mind numb

Nothing tests your mental strength like mind-numbing details, especially when you're tired. Yet the more you are _____, the more you should dig in and welcome it.

When I started my senior year thesis project for my engineering degree and realized the details that I had to provide to get my thesis approved, my brain started to hurt. I was tasked with solving a major breakage problem with a radiator tank made of 33 percent glass-filled nylon. It took a year of researching the operations of three separate plants and massive analysis before I solved the problem and turned in my thesis. It ended up getting an award, and the solution I discovered is now openly available to other engineers to study and implement.

What can you change about your attitude to become more detail focused?

_____

_____

_____

_____

_____

Be kind to people who are impolite to you

When people treat you poorly, it is tempting to stoop to their level and return the favor. When you have mental strength, you don't allow others to walk all over you, but you also do not have to be rude to them. Instead, treat impolite and cruel people with the same kindness you extend to everyone else. Don't allow their negativity to bring you down.

When I was in engineering school, one of my professors was very rude to me in front of my classmates because of my accent. I had not experienced anything like that from other educators, and it was quite embarrassing. His open criticism made me feel inadequate and brought on frustration. I never came back at him with any disrespect, but I kept a positive attitude, determined to perform at a high level in his class. I knew I had to do so in order to graduate, and I didn't want his negativity to delay me from reaching that goal.

What can you change about your attitude to not allow negativity to bring you down?

_____

_____

_____

_____

_____

Be accountable for your actions, no matter what

People are far more likely to remember how you dealt with a problem than they are to recall how it was created in the first place. So, instead of making an excuse, hold yourself _____. That will show that you care about results more than your ego.

One evening when I was under a lot of pressure and very stressed out, my teenage daughter asked me a question about an event. I responded to her in a rude way, and it didn't set well with her. I could see that I had offended her. I knew I had to be accountable for my actions, so I told her that I was sorry for my response and asked for her forgiveness. She granted it, the situation was resolved, and we were able to reengage right away.

CRAIG'S STORY

Craig was enormously popular at his workplace. Even a bitter rivalry there with, of all people, his younger brother didn't affect his likeability. If anything, it enhanced it, as did his character qualities of being straightforward and capable of owning up to his personal and professional shortcomings.

That was put to the test, however, when ongoing tension with his head supervisor caused what Craig believed to be a toxic work environment. That discomfort was only worsened when his competitive sibling took advantage of the situation and worked to undermine his brother's status in the company.

Craig honestly couldn't pinpoint the problem with his boss or its solution. Craig could've made excuses and hung in there just so his brother wouldn't win. But he set aside his ego and chose to resign. Craig's abrupt exit was a shock to his co-workers, even to those that knew a bit about what was going on behind the scenes. Yet Craig did not gossip or complain. He removed himself and proceeded onward to a new position, a different city, and a fresh start—empowered by the fact that he'd been accountable to his beliefs and maintained his integrity. "Most people are stronger than they know," he said to friends after his unexpected departure. "They just forget to believe in it sometimes."

Questions for application:

1. What do you think is the most challenging aspect of being self-accountable?

_____

_____

_____

_____

_____

2. How have you dealt with a professional or personal rival?

_____

_____

_____

_____

_____

3. When was the last time you cared about results more than your ego? Tell the story.

_____

_____

_____

_____

_____

To take an attitude that creates a "champion" mindset and *use it* to bring success to your life, you need something to fuel that process and propel you forward.

That fuel is belief—and there's nothing like it to make your Tuesday's turn out terrific every time.

Marvelous Monday—Attitude **Fill-in-the-Blank Answer Key:**

minds	coaching	grow
attitude	away	ego
mental	knowledge	manage
asset	seed	angle
perspective	ethic	challenged
weaknesses	confront	accountable
Mentorship	compete	

[3]

TERRIFIC TUESDAY
Belief

The Little Engine That Could by Watty Piper is a children's tale about a happy train loaded with food and toys. On the way to its destination, the train breaks down and becomes worried about all the kids who will not be able to play with the toys and eat all the yummies. Three different trains come by, but each one refuses to help because they are too proud, self-important, or tired.

Finally, a blue train shows up, and the toys desperately explain their situation and beg for help. The little engine thinks about all the good little boys and girls on the other side of the mountain who will not have any toys or food unless she helps. Despite its small size, the blue engine repeats the mantra, "I think I can, I think I can" over and over again as it pulls the train over the mountain. When it arrives, The Little Blue Engine repeats, "I thought I could. I thought I could."

The story's timeless lesson is simple and enduring: we can _____ great things when we believe—and there's no better way to follow up your Marvelous Monday attitude than with a Terrific Tuesday of confident belief!

This week, what mountain have you had to climb over? Share what happened.

_____

_____

_____

_____

_____

As the second day in the workweek, Tuesday is unique because it's the day that you want to create the **momentum** you need to carry you through the rest of the week. Ideally, Monday saw you getting off to a strong start. Your mindset is balanced and positive. Then Tuesday arrives with its sense of, "Okay, now how can I build upon that and keep this going?" That's where momentum comes in.

Simply defined, momentum is the impetus gained by a moving object. When you acquire and maintain momentum, you will _____ at your desired destination in a timely manner no matter how fast or slow others are moving around you. Likewise, you will have so much momentum that it would take something rather substantial to slow you down, much less stop you.

Momentum gets you where you need to go quickly and with pace. We need that on a Tuesday, don't we? Plus, momentum facilitates your belief and helps you to _____ it. As The Little Blue Engine repetitively told itself, "I think I can, I think I can," it created momentum. In the end, there was no mountain high enough to prevent it from making its delivery.

DANIEL'S STORY

Momentum was sometimes hard to come by for Daniel, and he knew the problem was of his own doing. As a young man, he had learned to take the hurts and mistakes of his past and mentally store them away behind a symbolic door in his mind. There they were safely repressed and denied, but they were never forgotten. Every time it seemed Daniel was poised to proceed forward, personally or professionally, a memory would reassert itself and hold him back. He was stuck in an unbalanced, negative mindset where guilt and shame from the past prevented him from moving forward in the present.

That's when his younger brother, Nick, stepped in. Daniel had always had a love-hate-love relationship with his sibling. Perhaps that was because both men knew the other better than anyone else did. So, when Nick challenged Daniel to confront those closeted wounds and regrets and bring them out into the open, he fiercely fought against it and his brother—at first. Yet as that mental door was opened, each encounter with the past brought internal revelation, and each revelation resulted in exponentially increasing freedom and peace of mind. That, in turn, freed Daniel to generate momentum and keep it going.

Today, the son of a pediatrician father and nurse mother is a renowned plastic surgeon, and he most recently returned to his native New Zealand after separating from his wife of nearly two decades. He remains involved with their two children, continues to deal with life's challenges head-on, and is working to solidify his practice in Auckland. He and Nick remain feisty, sometimes combative but forever inseparable friends. "Over the course of my long life, I have come to believe that we are bound forever to those with whom we share blood," Daniel said, "and while we may not choose our family, that bond can be our greatest strength."

Questions for application:

1. What negative or incorrectly used mindset is keeping you from having momentum in your life?

    _____

    _____

    _____

    _____

    _____

2. What or who can help you confront that mindset so you can gain and maintain momentum?

    _____

    _____

    _____

    _____

    _____

3. Who is your closest family member—and how has that person positively impacted your attitude or caused you to believe in yourself?

    _____

    _____

    _____

    _____

    _____

There are five attributes that will make your Tuesday both terrific and momentum filled—and they stem from **belief combined with action**. What you *do* will compel your belief forward and make it a reality! What does this require?

1. **Being steadfast.** Steadfastness means being resolutely or dutifully firm and unwavering. It speaks to having _____ and loyalty.

    I had to stay firm when I was attending GMI Engineering & Management Institute and was tempted to switch colleges. A bit homesick and overwhelmed with classwork, I thought it would be nice to be closer to home at Georgia Tech University. But I had been accepted at GMI with the help of some great people, not the least of whom was my mentor, Dr. David Green Jr. I decided to talk to him, and he was convinced I could do the work and handle all of the challenges at GMI. "Karockas," he said, "I brought you up here because I saw your work ethic and saw you overcome some things in your life, so I know you can do it. It is *in* you." With his exhortation, I chose to be loyal to him and faithful to what he declared was inside of me.

When you are steadfast, the self-belief that emerges is **self-efficacy.** An intense level of self-efficacy is supported by your steadfastness as you get a chance to witness your skills and talents in action. You see what you can do, and that removes _____. It shows you that you are likely better than you thought, and that you can do more. Still, even as Dr. Green told me what he saw in me, I nevertheless had to go do it. Once I witnessed my achievements, it made me confident, and my self-efficacy blossomed.

Self-efficacy is defined as belief in your own ability to succeed at a particular task or goal. On a scale of 1-10 (with 10 being the highest), how do you rate your current self-efficacy?

_____

Why did you give yourself that score?

_____

_____

_____

_____

_____

2. **Being immovable.** To be immovable is to remain fixed or unchangeable. It speaks to not _____, whatever the obstacle.

Starting around 2018, I observed a disturbing nationwide trend. It seemed as though many leaders were thinking about their own success without any regard to those who were following them. It was about getting all they could at the expense of others.

I had personally witnessed some self-centered leaders who made temporary gains in finances, position, and praise, and I could've become just as selfish. I could have acquired more things, made more money, and moved in greater circles of influence. Those temptations were there. But I had always believed in and taught servant leadership, and I knew that my leadership style was the right thing to do. The result? Those under my leadership at two different organizations grew and found fulfillment in their various areas of work and expertise.

When you are immovable, the self-belief that emerges is **self-control.** You become stationary in who you are and have control over the outside influences and forces that are trying to move you in the wrong direction. Self-control allows you to identify and understand your _____. It keeps you steady, not swaying from one place to the next. Self-control allows you to have the discipline you need to stay on course and succeed.

CLAIRE'S STORY

All of her life, Claire had wanted just one thing: to be able to love and live out her life with a husband and children. "I can grow old and have a family and fill my days with meaning," she once confessed to her brother, "knowing that each one matters." Yet her constant responsibilities running the family business and keeping it afloat against fierce competition seemed to make having such a life nothing more than a distant, impossible dream. Her situation appeared to be, in a word, immovable.

Then Claire was given an unexpected opportunity: a chance to take care of her sister-in-law's baby daughter, Rhiannon. Though their time together was brief, it allowed Claire to break away from the cares and burdens that both imprisoned and defined her, and she experienced firsthand what it was really like to have a child, at least from the standpoint of being an aunt. Claire began to believe that she could—and should—be a mother.

When she returned to work, Claire became immovable and unyielding in her determination to change her situation for the better. A massive restructuring and a complete revamp of her own job description was required, but they released Claire from enough of her vocational encumbrances so that she could start to develop a life outside of her workplace. As Claire believes in herself more, she is also gaining more control over herself, her circumstances, and her future. She now looks forward to finding someone with whom she can have a genuine relationship, fall in love, and have the family she has always desired.

Questions for application:

1. Tell the story of when you had to be immovable in order to move yourself in the right direction.

   _____

   _____

   _____

   _____

   _____

2. Claire's desire is for a family of her own. What is your most compelling yet unfulfilled desire personally or professionally?

_____

_____

_____

_____

3. What self-belief can you identify to allow the self-control you need to emerge so that you can start pursuing that desire?

_____

_____

_____

_____

3. **Being always abounding.** Abounding means to exist in large numbers or amounts. It speaks to being constantly _____ to the benefit of yourself and others.

Sometimes we need to abound to justify what we desire and achieve it. In Chapter 1, I shared about the time I was president of the Black Unity Congress in college and needed to secure extra funding for our plentiful work of supporting minority students in school and in civic life. Yet the school was less than five percent African American, so to get the money, we had to drive up membership. That meant becoming more inclusive to the entire student body and no longer remaining a segregated organization.

We upped our recruitment efforts, regularly setting up a table in the lunchroom. We did everything we could to find students who had a heart for what we stood for and wanted to help. What happened? We more than doubled our membership, including the addition of the student body president. A white man, his involvement sent a clear message that the Black Unity Congress was for everybody. We ended up having one of the highest budgets of any student government organization on campus.

When you are always abounding, the self-belief that emerges is **self-assurance.** That gives you the attitude that whatever it is that you want *will* happen. You actively look for a _____ result. Being always abounding feeds your mindset.

Self-assurance is defined as confidence in the validity and value of your own ideas or opinions. On a scale of 1-10 (with 10 being the highest), how do you rate your current self-assurance?

_____

Why did you give yourself that score?

_____

_____

_____

_____

_____

4. **Knowing that your efforts are not in vain.** If something is in vain, that means it was useless because it did not achieve anything. So, this speaks to being confident that what you are doing is _____ and will achieve great things.

All of us wonder at times if what we are doing is useful or just wasting time. Back in 1998, my church, Emmanuel: The Connection Church, launched a separate, non-profit organization called Victory Hope to help at-risk kids. Three days a week, we would pick up about 20 kids after school and bring them to our facility to tutor them, give life skills training, and essentially love on them. Each visit included a full, nutritious meal.

It was a lot of work for our crew of eight adults, and we sometimes questioned if we really were making a difference. But we were! Several of the kids who came through Victory Hope went on to do great things in life and fulfill their goals and dreams. Many got college degrees and worked good jobs. Others started businesses.

When you know that your efforts are not in vain, the self-belief that emerges is **self-confidence.** When you know that you are achieving something and that someone is or will benefit from your actions, it gives you confidence in your ability to facilitate _____ and the determination to keep going.

CHARLES' STORY

With an insatiable passion to do anything he could to help the downcast and disenfranchised, Charles looked to his ancestral legacy for inspiration. His third-great grandfather, Marcellus, was born in New Orleans, Louisiana in 1810 to a female slave and her white master who also happened to be head of the local parish government. Despite being the leader's son, Marcellus worked on his father's plantation and eventually had a family there himself, gaining a reputation for coming to the aid of his fellow slaves whenever they were in need. Stories passed down through the generations portrayed that no punishment was too harsh for Marcellus to bear and no injustice too great for him to fight.

So, when Charles was asked to return to New Orleans and set up a safe place for outcasts in the French Quarter to find shelter, food and clothing, and a chance to rehabilitate from the horrors only addiction can cause, he didn't hesitate. Determined that his efforts would not be in vain, Charles formed and maintained an alliance of the community's oft-divided factions, helping them work together to best serve the downtrodden and marginalized. He often told addicts who first arrived to begin recovery and treatment, "What you're feeling is a hunger. It will be unlike anything you've ever known. It will eat you from the inside. But you are in control—and make no mistake. We are family."

Over the course of nearly two decades, Charles' confident, self-belief infused efforts changed the lives of several thousand people who otherwise would've been lost and forgotten. He hopes his legacy will inspire future generations to serve. Today, Charles is retired and lives in New York City with the love of his life, Rebekah.

Questions for application:

1. Charles drew from the past for his inspiration. Who or what inspires you the most? Why?

_____

_____

_____

_____

_____

2. Pinpoint one thing you can do from that inspiration to be useful and facilitate change. Write it down as a goal.

_____

3. What self-belief can you identify to emerge the self-confidence you need to start pursuing that goal?

_____

_____

_____

5. **Fulfilling your actions as a labor of love.** A labor of love is a task done for pleasure, not reward. Wow! Isn't that profound? This speaks to selflessly _____ your work.

I have often said that love is a verb. It is an action, not a noun. When the COVID-19 pandemic first broke out, many people in our community in northern Alabama suffered from a lack of food. They were from all races and all ages, all demographics and all socioeconomic backgrounds, and I had never seen anything like it before. When I saw them standing in line for hours hoping to receive food and household supplies from a Christian ministry in Huntsville, it broke my heart and moved me to action. Ability Plus and Emmanuel: The Connection Church partnered to give out food boxes one Saturday morning. In all, we gave away a couple thousand boxes of non-perishable food: nuts, rice, cereal, and beans. It was hard, but incredibly rewarding, work. As we demonstrated love and cared for others, many people were blessed.

When you fulfill your actions as a labor of love, the self-belief that emerges is **self-esteem.** You cannot help but feel good about how you are impacting the situation and feel great about yourself for being involved in the work. _____ of yourself always elevates your self-esteem.

Every Tuesday, I compel my self-belief forward by doing *one thing* to brighten someone's day and intentionally do a kind act for them. Whatever it is, I am not looking to get anything back—and it does wonders for my self-esteem. When I help someone else, I feel better about myself. Doing that one thing every Tuesday builds and supports my momentum for the week. It gives me that little push to move me forward.

Self-esteem is defined as a realistic respect for, or favorable impression of, yourself. On a scale of 1-10 (with 10 being the highest), how do you rate your current self-esteem?

_____

Why did you give yourself that score?

_____

_____

_____

_____

_____

Genuine belief in yourself and in the destiny before you is essential—but it is not blind. It necessitates two primary characteristics that will give you the **vision** you need and that are sure to make your Tuesday terrific: knowledge and assent.

Knowledge is facts, information, and skills acquired through experience or education, and it requires the theoretical _____ and practice of those elements. My ability to gather knowledge is essential as a one-on-one leadership mentor because it's all about the people I'm serving. I must determine how their personalities fit with those they are leading, and I need to discern how they can better themselves so that those around them can be better.

Dr. Timothy Ifedioranma of Nigeria is a lawyer, pastor, bishop, and a congressperson for his country. One of my most successful leadership mentorship clients, I have visited Dr. Timothy no less than 18 times over a 20 year period. When I met with Dr. Timothy for a leadership conference in 2015, we discussed his passion to run for a seat in the Nigerian Congress. We talked about servant leadership and how that could relate to his roles in office as well as to his activities outside of the church community. We also explored how to structure his campaign. Was he going to speak solely to Christians, or was he going to try to get more people like Muslims to support his political run? He chose to be broad and invite everybody in. In Nigeria, it is common for politicians to become very wealthy. He did not want to be like them. He decided to dedicate himself to the whole community, put them first, and try to take care of all of their needs ahead of his own.

Dr. Timothy won that seat in Congress and, as of 2022, has remained in office. As I have continued to mentor him, he has done quite well and has had over 120 different churches operating under his authority. He has not only stayed the course, but he has also stayed true to his core values, who he is, and his "why" for living.

Your individual self-belief that is best supported by gaining and applying knowledge is **self-competency.** The acquisition and application of knowledge supports your self-competency by assessing your overall _____ to achieve desired outcomes as well as reflect skills you can gain through study and experience to complete a goal that helps fulfill your vision.

Self-competency is defined as the ability to shape your own personal and professional development largely independently of external influences. On a scale of 1-10 (with 10 being the highest), how do you rate your current self-competency?

_____

Why did you give yourself that score?

_____

_____

_____

_____

_____

Assent is an expression of approval or agreement, such as when two parties come together in _____ and harmony after mediation. I'll never forget when I assented to a friend so that I could learn how to best engage a specific group of business leaders. As an African American, I grew up in a culture that honors presenting yourself to others with a certain degree of confidence, even swagger. Two days prior to my presentation, I was preparing to show my consultation qualifications to members of the predominantly white business networking organization. My friend, who was white, saw me getting ready to discuss the honors and awards that I felt would validate me as a sound professional. He took me aside.

"Doc, you might not want to do it that way."

I was confused and a bit taken aback. "What do you mean?" I asked.

"They are going to think you are bragging on yourself. You're not going to convince them to work with you because they're going to think you're making it about you. They know who you are already."

I was instantly grateful, explaining to him that it is the norm in the African American culture to boldly let people know what we can do. "Matter of fact," I replied, "we give more respect to those who are doing certain things and can talk about it."

As I gave assent to my friend's sage advice, the presentation went well, the organization became a client, and the CEO of a contracting company who was at that presentation asked me to present a seminar to his team.

Your individual self-belief that is best supported by having assent is **value.** Expressing approval or agreement through assent supports value by equipping you to _____ to the cognitive, social, and moral development within a team.

Each Tuesday, I intentionally listen to or read about new leadership models or principles so that I can learn something new that I can apply to what I do. This increases my knowledge, provides opportunities to assent to new ideas, and feeds my overall vision.

Value is defined as your personal and professional relative worth, merit, or importance. On a scale of 1-10 (with 10 being the highest), how do you rate your current value?

_____

Why did you give yourself that score?

_____

_____

_____

_____

_____

Finally, your Terrific Tuesday is assured when you practice these four principles that inform and affirm your belief.

1. **Reliability.** Are you viewed by others as being trustworthy or as someone who consistently performs well? Being reliable to yourself and to those around you _____ your belief.

   In 2018, as a new board member of the Huntsville/Madison County Chamber of Commerce, I didn't just want to hold a seat on the board. I desired to be actively involved in things. I felt that the board had done a great job in the area of economic development. However, it could improve in engaging small businesses and upstart entrepreneurs by increasing their programs to them and by letting them know they are just as important as the military installations and other large businesses in the area. I suggested they provide scholarships and discounts to small business owners and entrepreneurs who could not afford some of the chamber's programs and even offer them full membership until they could grow their enterprises.

   To achieve this, I knew I had to show myself as being trustworthy to my fellow board members. I attended all of the meetings and was punctual. I constantly looked to add value to our conversations. I kept the private matters of the board confidential. My consistent commitment to operate with honesty and integrity was rewarded when I was appointed to the board's executive committee two years after first becoming a member.

   The self-belief of **dependability** is confirmed when you _____ yourself reliable. When you gain the sense that others can depend on you, you can depend on yourself.

Dependability is defined as your trustworthiness or constancy; the quality of being able to be relied on. On a scale of 1-10 (with 10 being the highest), how do you rate your current dependability?

_____

Why did you give yourself that score?

_____

_____

_____

_____

2. **Truth.** Do you live in accordance with fact or reality? What a great question—because being truthful _____ your belief.

Back in 1996, I was a young, maturing, and idealistic leader who firmly believed that people, in general, possessed an innate longing to develop themselves. I assumed that, given the opportunity, the majority of individuals would desire to gain the knowledge and work ethic to grow and succeed. Then I offered a series of small leadership seminars on self-development in areas such as career, finance, and mindset at my church. I was hoping our congregation members would embrace the chance to engage in self-growth and share details about the seminars with their friends and in their circles of influence. I was convinced that they would eagerly and joyfully want to better themselves.

But I was shocked. The vast percentage were utterly complacent. They were comfortable to see and experience life from the bottom up.

Wow, really? I thought. *I'd be eating this up and taking advantage of it.* But they weren't. They simply didn't want to change their attitude or their position. I had to accept that.

The self-belief of **veracity** is guaranteed by being truthful. With veracity, you will see and give _____ to the reality of what you and others expect in the future.

YUSUF'S STORY

When Yusuf stepped away from his position as a regent at a university in the southern United States, he had no plans to return. Though he felt he had served his students well in supervising their conduct and welfare, he had become frustrated with some of the bureaucracy he regularly encountered and was burned out. Yusuf wanted to live his own life. Problem was, he didn't really know what that meant apart from his service to college students.

Thankfully, he sought for, and found wisdom from, his friend, Camille. As a therapist, Camille was able to help Yusuf not only to identify his core passions as an individual, but she also led him down a path of desperately needed healing from a dark, troubled family past. As a result, Yusuf discovered his purpose and confirmed the truth that what he had been doing all along as a regent—being a servant leader to young adults—was, in fact, a fulfillment of his personal and professional "why."

Infused and energized, Yusuf resumed his role as a regent. His newfound veracity allowed him to work with increased credibility and integrity, allowing him to better deal with the pressures and red tape that came with the role. Best of all, his renewed focus on his student's well-being brought deep fulfillment. Of her ongoing influence in his life, Yusuf told Camille, "I won't forget what we set out to do, and I won't ever shy away from doing what needs to be done. If I stand against all that darkness, even if I do get chopped down, I know you're right there ahead of me."

Questions for application:

1. What have you had to either accept or step away from in order to gain renewed perspective about your passion and purpose?

_____

_____

_____

_____

_____

2. Who assisted you during that transition—and how did that person help?

_____

_____

_____

_____

_____

3. What self-belief can you identify to guarantee the truthfulness you need to acquire newfound veracity as you affirm and live out your "why?"

_____

_____

_____

_____

_____

3. **Ability.** How do you use your talents, skills, or proficiencies to benefit yourself and others? It's not enough to have ability. Properly and humbly executing your abilities _____ your belief.

In 2012, I had the privilege of traveling to Honduras with pastors and community and business leaders to speak at a crusade and leadership summit in the city of Puerto Cortés. The crystal blue waters of the Caribbean Sea provided the tropical backdrop for the outdoor portion of the event, and I marveled as the crowd gathered while kids rode bicycles or played in the dirt on the fringes. It was a large group of people, about 5,000 in all, many coming from long distances by bus.

As I spoke, an interpreter translated everything I said into Spanish. He also emulated my every movement. If I jumped, he jumped. If I spun, he spun. At one point, I took off from the stage and into the crowd, and he followed me the entire way. I was a madman, magnifying my ability to engage people and influence their behavior as I taught. Afterward, I received great feedback as many in attendance said their lives were changed for the better by what I said. Several declared that it gave them motivation and vision to pursue their dreams and goals. I was both thankful and quite humbled by it all.

The self-belief of **care** is declared by properly and humbly executing your abilities. Care brings an incredible sense of how you can _____ others to achieve their aspirations.

Care is defined as being concerned or solicitous; the quality of having thought or regard. On a scale of 1-10 (with 10 being the highest), how do you rate your current capacity to care?

_____

Why did you give yourself that score?

_____

_____

_____

_____

_____

4. **Strength.** Are you able to withstand great force or pressure exerted against you? Your solidity and endurance under trial _____ your belief.

In 2015, I came under attack as a CEO. An executive change took place at Ability Plus that upset several people. A delegation of nurses, state auditors, and even agents from the Internal Revenue Service came forth, questioning the services we were providing. The organization was investigated and scrutinized. Newly in charge, there was extraordinary pressure placed on me and my leadership team. We knew that we had been operating in integrity and firmly believed that things would eventually work out. We strongly held to our values and kept working hard and smart. In the end, we passed every audit, and the difficulties made us a better company.

The self-belief of **reliance** is maintained by being solid and having endurance under trial. You learn to _____ on. It's undeniably true. You are who you are under pressure.

What do I do every Tuesday to inform and affirm my belief? In the morning, I take a moment to visit my personal goal vision board in my office at home. The white board with pictures is a visual display of my vision, and I look at it and say aloud, "This is who you are." It is a brief but consistent weekly reminder that solidifies those goals and commitments I made to myself. It makes a world of difference in terms of maintaining momentum in my mindset.

ELYSE'S STORY

"This is who I am." Elyse has had to declare that to others more often than she would prefer since her decision to pivot from being a traditional caregiver to a practitioner of natural remedies for her patients. She was consistently criticized by some who balked at her refusal to utilize cannabis-related products because she insisted that far too little science had been done to actually prove its effectiveness. At the same time, Elyse was also condemned by others who thought the organic-focused treatments she did use were everything from unorthodox to borderline witchcraft.

At times, the attacks seemed too much to bear. Yet every time Elyse considered giving up, she dug in, reminded of her belief-driven vision to maximize safe, herbal solutions to help those in pain. She drew strength from the knowledge that she was effectuating her passion and discharging the purpose through her treatment methods—as well as from the consistent feedback from those she helped. One longtime client, Genevieve, put it this way: "Miss Elyse knows what she's doing. Her combination of ginger, turmeric, galangal, and cayenne in treatment of my sore back have worked wonders, and I haven't had to take one pharmaceutical. It's nothing short of supernatural. Most of all, Miss Elyse knows me and shows her care every time she sees me."

Such testimonials give Elyse momentum to carry on her work despite the naysayers, and such reliance has given her optimism regarding her future capacity and capability as a caregiver.

Questions for application:

1. Look back at your answer in Chapter 1 (the second truth about vision) regarding the last criticism you received and how it challenged you. What did you do to affirm your self-belief and hold up against the attacks that came your way?

   _____

   _____

   _____

   _____

   _____

2. Share how the testimony of someone else about you fed your strength during that trial?

_____

_____

_____

_____

_____

3. What self-belief can you identify to maintain the endurance you need to have reliance as you work to fulfill "who you are?"

_____

_____

_____

_____

_____

Belief has a final and enduring benefit: a recognition and release of potential. A key component of any movie worth its salt (at least by my standards) is the "chase scene." It's that vital sequence when the good guy—through extraordinary risk, daring heroics, and the gratuitous use of a stuntman—gets away from the bad guy unscathed. It's cinematic artistry.

Your week is made better by chase scenes—as long as you're the one in hot pursuit of continued progress and excellence. That requires seeing and going after your potential.

What a Wonderful Wednesday it is going to be!

Terrific Tuesday—Belief **Fill-in-the-Blank Answer Key:**

accomplish	useful	show
arrive	change	guarantees
fulfill	enjoying	credence
faithfulness	Giving	declares
doubt	understanding	help
yielding	ability	maintains
parameters	consensus	hold
plentiful	contribute	
positive	confirms	

Notes

[4]

WONDERFUL WEDNESDAY
Potential

"The wealthiest spot on this planet," Dr. Myles Munroe wrote in his book, *Releasing Your Potential*, "is not the oil fields of Kuwait, Iraq, or Saudi Arabia. Neither is it the gold and diamond mines of South Africa, the uranium mines of the Soviet Union, or the silver mines of Africa. Though it may surprise you, the richest deposits on our planet lie just a few blocks from your house."

Munroe then revealed that place to be the local cemetery or graveyard. There, he said, buried beneath the soil within the walls of those sacred grounds, are:

- Dreams that never came to pass.
- Songs that were never sung.
- Books that were never written.
- Paintings that never filled a canvas.
- Ideas that were never shared.
- Visions that never became reality.
- Inventions that were never designed.
- Plans that never went beyond the drawing board of the mind.
- Purposes that were never fulfilled.

"Our graveyards," he concluded, "are filled with potential that remained potential."
What wisdom! Unrealized potential is just that: unrealized.

One of the most effective ways to reveal your unrealized potential is to write your own epitaph (the words people would read on your cemetery headstone). Do that here. Limit it to just a few sentences.

Herein lies _____ *(your name). I am to be remembered for...*

_____

_____

_____

_____

_____

Drawing once again from the world of science, potential energy is the prospective vitality held by an object because of its position relative to other objects, stresses within itself, or other factors. The power is there—but it is not manifested until it is _____.

One comparison I like to make uses the formula for gravitational potential energy (mass x gravity x height) related to sales within a business: leads (mass) x activity (gravity) x booking appointments (height) results in sales (potential energy) being released.

Potential needs a catalyst in order to be _____. As Dr. Munroe rightly said, "A seed, until it is released, is only the promise of a tree."

In my "Point of Potential" (POP) Equation for Success seminars, I take out an apple, cut it in half to expose the seeds at the core, and hold it out to the audience. "We all see this apple," I teach, "but it came from a seed. Inside each seed is a tree, and inside a tree are more apples. Everything starts from the seed, and it is the seed that has the potential to produce a tree that will produce more apples."

"If the seed is not placed into the ground where it can germinate and be watered and nourished, it does not grow. It's promised potential is not released," I tell attendees. "That means we have to plant the seeds of potential that reside at our core. We have to water ourselves through trainings, research, study, and education. We have to sacrifice. Only then can a tree grow. Then, when it does, there will be a time that tree will need to be pruned. We will need to cut back, getting rid of anything or anyone that isn't doing us any good, in order to bear more fruit."

Look at the epitaph you just wrote for yourself. What seed of unrealized potential does it reveal to you?

_____

_____

_____

_____

_____

The POP equation I created is **S + WE x W = POP**—or **S**tart + **W**ork **E**thic x **W**hy = **P**oint **of** **P**otential. Potential always starts somewhere. My start traces all the way back to growing up in the projects and living in government housing in small town Alabama.

When I was 15, I was sitting in the kitchen one afternoon with my mother, Johnnie, when she planted the seed of potential in my life. She was cooking, and I was telling her how I was thinking about becoming a doctor. She was a nurse, and I had been reading her medical books with keen interest.

"Karockas," she declared, "you are smart. You can be anything in the world—except president of the United States. Do not let what you see dictate what you could be."

That was quite the proclamation to make back then to an African American boy from the projects, and I can't help but laugh today at her qualifier: Barack Obama has proven that even our nation's highest political office can be attained by a person of color.

My mother's words encouraged me, and though I did not become a doctor, I have attained a doctorate—and achieved so much more than even I thought possible in my roles as a pastor, business leader, and entrepreneur. I may not have had many of the advantages other people have enjoyed, but I had a launching pad, thanks to my mother. I used it to motivate myself.

That said, I still had to take my start and add a relentless _____ ethic multiplied by my fully defined "_____" (to lead, teach, train, and empower people to reach their destiny by helping them to maximize their potential) in order to reach my own Point of Potential—that place where my potential was released and became a reality.

Think back to your childhood and identify a moment when you realized your potential. Tell the story.

_____

_____

_____

_____

For me, it was, "Do not let what you see dictate what you could be." What takeaway message about your potential came from your story?

_____

_____

_____

_____

_____

Have you lived up to that potential, fallen short of it, or exceeded it? Explain.

_____

_____

_____

_____

_____

On Sunday, we began the week by establishing our vision. We set our attitude on Monday and infused our belief on Tuesday. What better way, then, to meet and overcome the traditional "hump" day of Wednesday and make it wonderful than by igniting and fulfilling our potential?

Once more, your mindset is key; specifically, one of meditation where you _____ your thoughts to see and rehearse the actions you _____. When you are truly *present* with your mindset, you'll discover that your brain can hardly tell the difference between what you rehearse in advance and experience in real time. One automatically _____ the other.

There are five attributes of a Wonderful Wednesday that will foster your meditation and direct you toward the release of your potential.

1. **Train your brain not to be a record of your past, but a map to your future**

    Our brains record information that is stored in our conscience until we are challenged or called upon to use it. When that happens, many recall negative messages—"You can't do this." "This is too hard." "No one has ever done that before." "My family failed at this, so I will, too."—which cause them to feel _____ and often places them on a path of failure.

    Therefore, you must place new, positive information into the hard drive of your brain that foretells and inspires your success and maps out your brighter future. "Nothing can stop me. I can do all things!" "Greatness is inside of me. It will just take some work to get it out of me." "I will look at every hill as something I can get over." "If I keep moving forward, I will profit from it sooner or later."

    Though challenges are inevitable, this new mapping of your brain shows that you have or will overcome, conquer, and succeed. One of the most remarkable things you have the power to do is literally *rewrite* your brain. Scientists refer to this as neuroplasticity: the ability of neural networks in the brain to change through growth and reorganization in response to new situations or to changes in their environment. For example, when individuals with an addictive behavior make consistent, ongoing alterations in their thinking and behavior, the brain closes down the old neural pathways that enabled that addiction and opens up new neural pathways that support ongoing sobriety or abstinence.

    More than mere willpower, your positive thoughts and choices _____ your brain. As this happens, your brain heals itself!

How does this revelation about neuroplasticity and your ability to influence it make you feel about your unrealized potential? Why?

_____

_____

_____

_____

_____

As a church pastor, I faced a situation where I had to train my brain to not be a record of the past. We needed to move to a new, bigger location. Anytime we had done this before, the move was met with much pain and disappointment. People left. Tithes and offerings decreased. Many who stayed didn't feel we needed to make the change because they were very comfortable where they were. Everything was received by the congregation as a negative—and that stuck in my brain. I was overwhelmed with anxiety, and I even wondered if everyone was going to leave this time.

I had to change my mindset and see the church relocation in a positive, successful way in order to create a map of progress toward the future. Three times every week, I went to the new building, sat in my car, and meditated. Next, I walked inside and went into every classroom, envisioning the teaching that was going to take place. I stood in the main sanctuary and imagined the messages to come and how they were going to be received with enthusiasm. I went beyond visualization, speaking aloud the positives I wanted to see happen in each and every space in that building. I saw our people joyful, happy, and embracing the move as an opportunity for us to expand our outreach and grow in our faith.

As I did this, my brain's neural pathways changed. Negative thinking was vanquished. Positive thinking was established. That influenced how I felt and behaved. Today, my church is thriving, and I continue to walk through the building once a week meditating and speaking out loud. I call into existence those things which be not as though they were, and I declare that a positive future will come to pass.

Can you see yourself doing what I did? Why or why not?

_____

_____

_____

_____

_____

2. Teach your body what the future feels like emotionally ahead of the actual experience

In addition to addressing our thoughts and behavior, we must train ourselves emotionally. This improves our self-esteem: how we _____ about ourselves.

Incredibly, the average person has as many as 60,000 thoughts a day—and the vast majority of them, 80 percent, are negative.[5] You can offset this trend in your thinking by emotionally esteeming your current goals and your future expectations about them _____ your present reality. See it, believe it, and act as if it has already happened. Tell yourself, "Yes, I can! I can feel this way. I *deserve* to feel this way."

I'll never forget my first board meeting as CEO at Ability Plus. My body was feeling so much anxiety about what could go wrong. The organization had been in disarray. The previous leader had not been forthright with the board. They were having a crisis of trust. Previously, board meetings had involved long hours of bickering. The overall culture was bad from all of the dysfunction, and I was still feeling disappointed and frustrated about all of this stemming from my time as the organization's chief operating officer. As CEO, I was in a position to change things and make a difference, but I was nervous and fearful.

So, I had to refocus my energy and mindset to believe and experience a positive, productive meeting before it occurred. As I had as pastor at the church, I meditated for about 15 minutes the night before the board meeting and again about an hour before the start of the meeting. I went into the boardroom and thought about how fun and productive it was going to be. I pictured smiles on everyone's faces. I engaged the theater of my mind to visualize a positive outcome. That changed my emotional outlook.

That first meeting went well, and the board meetings that followed it got even better. We went to work to reform damaged processes, rebuild broken trust, and change the culture.

TARYN'S STORY

A vivid imagination had always been a defining characteristic of Taryn's personality. From her days as a girl peering into the fireplace and longing for a visit from her imaginary friend to nights staring at the broken clock on the mantle and pretending to be a little queen, Taryn accepted her present realities and futuristic fantasies equally and with abandon. That she, therefore, demonstrated sharp intelligence and an open-minded nature as a young adult, female executive was simply an extension of her fanciful psyche.

Taryn sometimes struggled, though, to apply that temperament to her emotions. Negativity could gnaw away at her self-esteem and stifle her creative leanings when it came to seeing the potential of where she could go as a leader. Yet when she began leveraging her lively imagination and valuing her current goals and expectations by envisioning, perceiving, and operating as if they had already been achieved, Taryn experienced a breakthrough personally and professionally. It was a slow path, but in time, she developed herself and is now recognized as one of the most accomplished and courageous executives in her company. Taryn often tells her colleagues, "A door once opened may be stepped through in either direction," as an indication of her ongoing, visionary, and forward-thinking optimism.

Questions for application:

1. How would you characterize your own imagination? Why?

_____

_____

_____

_____

_____

2. Think about a professional challenge you are facing right now. In what ways can you broaden or apply your imagination to address that situation?

_____

_____

_____

_____

_____

3. What is the first thing that comes to mind when you read Taryn's words, "A door once opened may be stepped through in either direction?"

_____

_____

_____

_____

_____

3. **Transform your attitude to feel empowered even when you have not received recognition.**

It's easy to wait for someone to provide us with a sense of accomplishment before we feel good about our ability, efficiency, or strength. But it's far better to see yourself as accomplished and empowered on the canvas of your imagination _____ the success is manifested. That way, you will feel that the capability is inside of you from the very start.

When I launched my work as a leadership consultant, I knew that I had to feel capable of doing a great job before I ever did a single seminar or coaching session. I could not afford to wait until someone said, "Good job, Karockas." I needed to feel empowered that a good job was going to happen. Once more, it started with meditation. Many times, I envisioned myself commanding a crowd like Les Brown or engaging an audience like John C. Maxwell. I'd tell myself, *They can't beat Doc Rock!* I saw myself walking off stage with people saying, "Man, that dude was awesome!"

This did not flow from any sense of arrogance. It came solely from the perspective of building my self-awareness and self-confidence. In doing so, the aspect of my potential that I released was open-mindedness. I believed and felt that I was capable of consulting and coaching, and that transformation of my attitude contributed to my success.

What can you start doing every Wednesday to become more open-minded about your potential?

_____

_____

_____

_____

_____

4. **Conform your mindset to feel abundant before you receive wealth.**

It's also just as easy to wait until our bank account, assets, environment, or social circles look more favorable before we feel we are abundant. That doesn't need to be the case. Your abundance can be _____ in the mind before it is played out on the daily court of life. You can walk with your head up and your shoulders back as you develop a holistic sense of abundance in advance so that you feel you have everything you need to achieve what you want.

In 2013, I felt that the church I was leading had to alter some essential outreach philosophies to become more inclusive. I wanted to present our ministry from a more contemporary point of view, reaching people where they were with grace and love instead of with judgment. Vast numbers of the congregation, however, favored tradition and did not want to change. As they left the church, giving dramatically decreased, leaving it in a financial bind.

Yet even with our monetary abundance threatened, I refused to go forward with a mindset of lack. I told myself each day that the condition of our cash flow was great and that we were going to experience more opportunity and prosperity as we stayed the course. Over time, that is exactly what happened.

MARC'S STORY

As a retail logistics manager for a modest little hauling company. Marc saw himself and his financial situation as ordinary and unlikely to change. Other than his interests in television (he helped form a club about his favorite show) and music (that club formed a band that performed cover songs of his favorite classic rock group), Marc lived alone in an apartment and had no professional or monetary ambitions beyond his current state. It wasn't that he was settling. Internally, Marc desired to be and have more. He just didn't perceive that it was possible.

That changed when Linda, one of his fellow club members, talked to him about abundance. She shared how her mindset had changed once she became aware that she could pursue and get everything she wanted to accomplish what she desired. She explained that she had to see herself as prospering before she could begin to prosper. With Linda as a living example and continued inspiration, Marc transformed his thinking and started to recognize his full potential personally and vocationally. He sought and received a promotion at work, and he began saving money for a new, previously unimaginable goal: to buy a home.

Within two years, Marc financed and moved into that house—with Linda. The inseparable pair had found what he called a strange magic together and fallen in love. Her optimism, perspective, and care remain a foundational stone in Marc's life. He certainly has received and become more than he could've ever imagined.

Questions for application:

1. For Marc, it was a promotion and a home. What are two things you want but do not feel it is possible to have?

_____

_____

2. For each one, what can you change about your sense of abundance to *believe* you can have them?

_____

_____

_____

_____

3. For each one, what is the first thing you can *do* to begin pursuing them?

_____

_____

_____

_____

4. How can someone you love help you achieve those goals?

_____

_____

_____

_____

5. **Adjust your awareness to feel accepted and respected even when others haven't made you feel that way.**

All of us like to "feel the love" from those around us, so much so that we may wait to feel that way about ourselves until someone else shows it to us. But you should accept and respect yourself anyway _____ having to feel loved by others, acting as if you have already received that appreciation.

I recall struggling with this early in my business consultation career. I wanted to be loved by others, especially those I perceived as being ahead of me. When I didn't readily "feel the love," it fostered doubt in my mind. *Am I supposed to be in this room? Does everybody want me to be here? Do I deserve to be here?* I had to act as though I knew I was supposed to be in the room. *I'm here*, I told myself. *I can't wait for them to come over to me. I have to believe and behave as if everybody is waiting to hear my name, talk to me, and ask questions about my expertise.* Acceptance and respect had to come from me first. I had to give both to myself.

Did I ever have to overcome a sense that I was only pretending to feel loved or "faking it 'til I made it?" Sure, a little bit. But in the end, I came to the awareness that my inner acceptance and self-respect were real and just as significant as though I'd received it from others. Of course, there were those who let me "feel the love," and that was great. But I got to the point where I didn't need that in order to feel like I belonged with those people.

Every Wednesday morning and evening, I foster meditation and direct myself toward the release of my potential by taking time to look at my vision board and think about the grand scale items such as a leadership development center for Vision Excellence Company, tripling company growth for Ability Plus, a new ministry facility for my church, and getting and keeping myself in great physical shape. I see these goals as though they were already completed so that I can share the benefits of those achievements with others.

In my meditation, I use verbalization, visualization, and internalization. These three encompass and address the basic components of an *experience* shaped by words spoken out loud, emotions felt as real, and images seen on the canvas of my imagination. I am convinced that experiences such as these have the most potent impact on the belief system that controls our lives.

What can you start doing every Wednesday to adjust your awareness to feel more accepted and respected?

_____

_____

_____

_____

_____

What is excellence? It is the quality of being outstanding, truly the best, at everything you do. Different people measure excellence in different ways, but it is always that which sets its standard for a particular area—and the characteristics of a Wonderful Wednesday designed to release your potential revolve around your own pursuit of excellence.

Be intentional by allocating attention to your purpose. Your purpose—your "why" in life that is centered around your gifts and passions—does not just happen. It is something that requires your daily attention. When you allocate time to do what is needed to pursue your purpose, you automatically _____ your potential and accelerate toward excellence. One great way to do this is to daily review and speak your purpose out loud.

I remember being in an executive staff meeting where we discussed the industry standard for business excellence. I noted how many companies were being allowed to operate with low excellence in the area of professionalism. We decided that, though apathy was an easier path, we wanted to do everything we could to operate at the highest level of professional excellence.

We developed a strategy to be the most professional company in our industry. Surprisingly, we were confronted by naysayers who mistakenly thought we were just trying to make ourselves seem more "special" than our competitors. These naysayers had a lack of confidence, purpose, and direction that caused them to think the way that they did. Yet it was not our intention to put anyone down. We simply wanted to set the bar high for ourselves and go after it. As a result, our executive team was challenged to look at average as the enemy to great, and their mindsets changed to look, act, and move toward being the very best.

JESSICA'S STORY

Jessica knew and lived her "why." As a school nurse, her passion was to care for her students' physical needs as well as to encourage them through their ever-evolving emotional challenges. But her friend, David, a teacher, did not have such confidence in his "why." He told her that he loved being an educator, and his pupils certainly liked and appreciated his efforts in the classroom, but his subconscious thoughts betrayed him. David often confided in Jessica about his vivid, sometimes seemingly outlandish dreams of being a traveler, going from one adventure to the next, and writing about it. In fact, David kept a journal and sketches of his dreams because what they represented was so meaningful to him.

Late one afternoon as they sat together outside the teacher's lounge and gazed at the silhouettes of the scarecrows in the cornfields adjacent to the school, Jessica confronted David. "You speak longingly of exotic and faraway places and things like they are a part of who you truly are. Answer me this. If you had never become a teacher, would you be traveling everywhere, as though through time and space, living out those wonderful fantasies you write and draw?"

David looked down at his timepiece, a simple silver watch on a chain, and smiled. "Without question, yes, I would."

Jessica didn't hesitate. "Then you know what you need to do."

At the end of the semester, David left the school and embarked on the literal fulfillment of his dreams. As a successful travel author, he later published his "Journal of Impossible Things," chronicling his many trips and adventures. It was dedicated to Jessica.

Questions for application:

1. It undoubtedly took some risk for David to fulfill his purpose. How does thinking about pursuing your "why" make you feel? Excited? Afraid? Overwhelmed?

   _____

   _____

   _____

   _____

   _____

2. Why do you believe you feel that way about your "why?"

_____

_____

_____

_____

_____

3. What should you do about it?

_____

_____

_____

_____

_____

Be expectant by aiming past your expectations. I've always said, "Shoot for the galaxies and maybe you will land on the moon." It's an attitude that came from being raised near Huntsville, Alabama, also known as the "Rocket City" because it is the home of the United States Space and Rocket Center, the National Aeronautics and Space Administration's Marshall Space Flight Center, and the United States Army Aviation and Missile Command. It's always been a place where progressive industries in aerospace, defense, and biotech have informed its culture.

As a kid, I remember going to the Space and Rocket Center during an all-day, fifth grade field trip. I didn't know it was a replica then, but I was amazed when I saw the Saturn 5 rocket that took us to the moon towering high into the crystal blue Alabama sky. When the tour guides spoke about how everyone at the Space and Rocket Center had to be innovative in technology and communications, something was stirred within me to think that nothing was impossible. They went beyond the limits of what many expected in sending humans to the moon. Why couldn't I do the same in my life?

I've found that many people tend to set their goals so low they can't help but hit them all. However, to unleash your potential and achieve excellence, you must _____ yourself above and beyond where you think you can go.

In general, have you set your goals so low you can't help but hit them? Be honest.

_____

_____

_____

_____

_____

Choose two professional goals. What can you change about each one, so they aim past your expectations?

1. _____

   _____

   _____

2. _____

   _____

   _____

Be proactive by having a strong vision for the long term. You must constantly be on high alert with your vision. Why? Because vision always puts you beyond your capacity, but never beyond your potential to see, plan, and produce your desired future with imagination. When you are proactive with your vision, it gives you renewed _____ to keep pressing toward your potential.

As CEO of Ability Plus, I was proactive with the vision I had of owning our own building with offices and a career center. We had rented building space for years, and even during hard times with our operations and finances, we kept the vision to own at the forefront. In 2017, we purchased our own building that provided us with the necessary offices, meeting rooms, and campus space that we didn't have before, enabling us not just to continue but to expand our mission to those we serve.

CAREY'S STORY

When it comes to having proactive vision, Carey has learned three overriding lessons. Don't turn your back. Don't look away, and don't blink! A young photographer with the mindset and curiosity of a detective, Carey was not naturally inclined toward risk. She generally favored playing it safe. Yet when she saw an opportunity to open and run an antiquarian bookshop with her best friend's brother, Larry, Carey knew it would fulfill a vision she'd always secretly harbored. She liked old books, Carey said, because they made her feel sad in a good way. But launching and running the shop would force her to go beyond her perceived capacity.

It took a lot of time, all of an entire year packed with unexpected challenges to solve and obstacles to overcome, yet Carey and Larry took them on. She said it sometimes felt as if there was something working against them, just waiting to creep up and send them into oblivion. But in the end, Carey and her partner courageously conquered them all. They didn't blink—and the result was the bookshop of her dreams becoming a reality. Today, it thrives, as do Carey and Larry as business partners and as a committed couple.

"A friend once told me that people don't understand time. It's complicated," she said, "especially when pursuing a vision. But I've learned that I'm clever, and I'm listening. When it comes to pressing toward my potential, I'm always listening and learning, and I'm convinced that neither demons nor angels can stand in the way of me achieving what I want when I put my mind to it."

Questions for application:

1. What natural inclination do you have to challenge in order to engage your proactive vision? Why does it need to change?

2. When you read about Carey's confidence in herself, how does it make you feel about your own self-confidence? Why?

3. List two ways you feel you are clever and/or a good listener, then share how that encourages you to go beyond your perceived capacity.

    a. _____

    _____

    _____

    _____

    _____

    b. _____

    _____

    _____

    _____

    _____

Be thirsty to invest in your capacity by obtaining, retaining, and improving your knowledge and skills. Continual education and self-improvement are essential to growing _____ the fulfillment of your potential. It is necessary that you stay on top of industry changes and embrace a growth mindset at all costs.

I had already obtained several degrees when I decided to enter the graduate school business and leadership certificate program at Vanderbilt University in 2015. Some people insisted that I already had enough education—and that may have been true. But I didn't have the proper knowledge that was necessary to get me to the next level in my potential. Through this program, I received training in conflict resolution, change management, and other critical skills. I also gained additional business and leadership acumen.

To promote the pursuit of excellence in my life, I make sure I learn something new each and every Wednesday. It may be small, and it doesn't take much time from the day, but it is always something that I know will improve and extend my skills.

What can you start doing every Wednesday to invest in your capacity professionally or personally?

_____

_____

_____

_____

_____

Once you have begun using meditation and focusing on excellence to release your potential in the middle of your work week, the last way to guarantee a Wonderful Wednesday is by doing everything you can to inspire your productivity by following these three principles.

1. **Limit your external distractions.**

   Two Major League Baseball hall of famers—Yogi Berra, catcher for the New York Yankees, and Hank Aaron, home run hitting king for the Milwaukee Braves, were playing in the 1957 World Series. Berra, who was notorious for his ceaseless chatter, used to pick up his teammates while distracting the opposing team's batters. As Aaron came up to the plate, Berra said, "Henry, you're holding the bat wrong. You're supposed to hold it so you can read the trademark."

   Aaron didn't say anything. Instead, he slammed the next pitch into the left field bleachers. After rounding the bases and stepping on home plate, Aaron looked at Berra. "I didn't come up here to read," he said.[6]

   Hank Aaron would not be distracted from the task at hand, and neither should you. I have put into practice four easy to understand (yet difficult to execute) ways to limit distractions.

   a. Manage your phone/tablet/laptop: Treat your electronic devices primarily as a tool for productivity, not an instrument of entertainment. Most of us have a tendency to be distracted and amused by our devices, often utilizing them as stress releasers. That's why it is best to purposefully curtail entertainment and target using your devices on tasks that help you achieve your goals and dreams. This is hard to do because it decreases the feeling of satisfaction and comfort you get when devices are employed for other purposes.

What can you change today to better manage your electronic devices so that you will maximize your potential?

_____

_____

_____

_____

_____

b. Manage people: Always be open and show respect to everyone, but don't allow anyone to control or misuse your time. Many people have good intentions but are bad time managers when interacting with others. Yet you must manage every relationship with respect to the milestones and priorities at hand. This is difficult because we generally don't want others to think that we don't care about them or don't want to take time for their concerns.

What can you change today to better manage the people in your life so that you will maximize your potential?

_____

_____

_____

_____

_____

c. Manage your work and study space: Work is the necessary activity that enables you to achieve success, so it must be given proper precedence and respect. Your work or study space must be guarded as the sanctuary it is to get this activity moving and keep it going. This is not easy to do because other things tend to come up to interrupt or supersede your prioritization of work and study.

What can you change today to better manage your work and study space so that you will maximize your potential?

_____

_____

_____

_____

_____

d. Manage noise: Noise comes your way every day, usually in the form of people or fun, and it clamors for your time and attention. The best way to silence it is to intentionally review your daily tasks and see what goals need to be accomplished to fulfill those tasks. As you keep the big picture in front of you, you are able to give it preference over the noise. This is difficult because it requires great discipline.

What can you change today to better manage the noise in your life so that you will maximize your potential?

_____

_____

_____

_____

_____

2. **Identify your priorities.**

"A weakness of all human beings," inventor and entrepreneur Henry Ford once stated, "is trying to do too many things at once. That scatters effort and destroys direction. It makes for haste, and haste makes waste. So, we do things all the wrong ways possible before we come to the right one. Every now and then, I wake up in the morning headed toward that finality with a dozen things I want to do. I know I can't do them all at once."

Knowing how to pinpoint and do "first things first" is essential to setting your priorities—and I've learned that the ABCDE Method is a powerful priority setting technique that you can use every single day. Basically, it is a to-do list on steroids, and its power lies in its simplicity because it's so action oriented. All you do is start with a list of everything you want to accomplish for the coming day, then employ the ABCDE Method.

"A" items are most important.

"B" items only have minor consequences.

"C" tasks have no consequences.

"D" indicates items you can delegate.

"E" shows tasks that you can eliminate.

In my office at the start of each day, I look at my action items and break them down into four categories: three for the organizations that I lead and one for personal tasks. Next, I prioritize each list using ABCDE. This can get tricky because each ranking is based on the various criticalities, the items of extreme importance, for that given day. This is vital because each day is different and fluid. Something categorized as "C" yesterday might be an "A" today. Unexpected meetings or events can become more important than other action items. Dealing with such criticalities and the fluidity of each individual day is the strength of the ABCDE Method. It becomes a tool that allows you to have the flexibility you need to be most productive.

TONY'S STORY

Tony was an artist who specialized in trying to do too many things at once. Whether it was a portrait or an abstract, he often found inspiration for his paintings in dreams or simply on a whim. Tony would respond—only to be distracted by another spark of genius. The result was canvas after canvas left unfinished, and he was rarely pleased with those he did complete. Worst of all, Tony's self-confidence as a creator was undermined. He often felt at war with himself, frustrated, and even hopeless. He constantly wondered, *Will anyone ever see and appreciate my work, much less want to purchase it?*

That's when Amelia, an unexpected visitor to his studio, changed Tony's perspective and his life. As she openly admired Tony's work, he became confident enough to share his problem with her. Over coffee, he found himself revealing to Amelia how his inspiration manifested itself. "I can hear the voices of the colors speaking to me," he said. "I can hear the world yelling at me to capture its mysteries."

Amelia accepted Tony's ravings not as those of some manic madman, but as expressions of the type of artist he was. "All you need to do," she encouraged Tony, "is learn to harness those inspirations, then organize and prioritize them so that you can focus on one piece at a time. Then you can finish each one to your satisfaction."

In the months that followed, Amelia and Tony became close friends, and she helped hold him accountable to a new mindset and attitude of creative productivity. Tony completed his paintings, and his self-confidence soared. His art was not only seen and appreciated, it sold—but there was one piece he kept for himself. It depicted a bouquet of sunflowers with the inscription "for Amy" on the vase. Tony still cites it as his most important work.

Questions for application:

1. In the past year, when have you tried to do too many things at once?

_____
_____
_____
_____
_____

2. How did that situation make you feel about yourself and your ability? Why?

_____
_____
_____
_____
_____

3. Apply the ABCDE Method right now to tomorrow's tasks. Write it out here.

a. _____
_____

b. _____
_____

c. _____
_____

d. _____
_____

e. _____
_____

3. **Have a method for measuring productivity.**

Former athlete Deion Sanders once played as an outfielder for the Atlanta Braves and a cornerback for the Atlanta Falcons at the same time. He is the only athlete to have hit a home run in Major League Baseball and scored a touchdown in the National Football League in the same week—so he knows a little something about productivity.

While growing up in Fort Myers, Florida, Sanders met several would-be athletes. "I call them Idas," he said. "'If I'da done this, I'd be making three million today,' or 'If I'da practiced a little harder, I'd be a superstar.' They were as fast as me when they were kids, but instead of working for their dreams, they chose drugs and a life of street corners. When I was young, I had practice; my friends who didn't went straight to the streets and never left." He concluded, "We don't need any more Idas."[7]

You'll know that you are being productive—and not being another "Ida"—by employing these methods to track your productivity.

- Establish a baseline.
- Define and measure tasks.
- Set clear objectives and goals.
- Identify benchmarks and targets.
- Follow your individual progress.

At General Motors, I oversaw a project to retool an assembly line with electric torque guns so that they would be implemented on two of the three standard work shifts: day, evening, and overnight. Much had to be done in the established baseline of three months to complete the first phase of the retooling, from training to the ordering and installation of equipment. We set weekly benchmarks for everyone, and I had to keep an overall log of activities to monitor our progress and keep us on schedule. All five tracking methods were employed.

There were a few unforeseen challenges that arose from some of the workers being skeptical of the new process, but we overcame them by listening to one another, asking and answering detailed questions, and working together. The project was fully and successfully completed within the baseline.

Have you ever said to yourself, "If I'da done this...things might be different today?" Tell the story.

_____

_____

_____

_____

_____

Name one task you can begin to measure this week using all five of these tracking methods.

_____

_____

In the end, I plug all of these things into my personal POP equation to continually strive for my Point of Potential. As a result, I don't just get over my "hump" days—I launch over them like a kid speeding his bike to a hill and ramping himself up and beyond it.

Yet there are days, more than I'd like to admit, where I need an infusion of confidence to make it through to the other side—and that is where your Triumphant Thursday comes into play.

Wonderful Wednesday – Potential **Fill-in-the-Blank Answer Key:**

released	feeds	experienced
realized	average	without
work	rewrite	unleash
"why"	feel	stretch
focus	above	hope
want	before	toward

Notes

_____

_____

_____

_____

_____

_____

_____

_____

_____

_____

_____

_____

_____

_____

_____

_____

_____

_____

_____

5

TRIUMPHANT THURSDAY
Confidence

Confidence can come from something tangible. The noted American artist, John Singer Sargent, was considered the leading portrait painter of his generation, creating nearly 900 oil paintings and more than 2,000 watercolors, as well as countless sketches and charcoal drawings. He once painted a panel of roses that was highly praised by critics. A small picture, Sargent refused to sell it. He considered it his best work and was very proud of it.

Whenever he was deeply discouraged and doubtful of his abilities as an artist, he would look at it and remind himself, "I painted that." Then his confidence and ability would come back to him.[8]

Confidence can also come from an _____ mindset. John McKay, a well-known college and professional football coach for over 25 years, wrote about the supreme confidence of legendary University of Alabama football coach Bear Bryant. "We were out shooting ducks, and finally, after about three hours, here comes one lonely duck. The Bear fires. And that duck is still flying today. But Bear watched the duck flap away, looked at me and said, 'John, you are witnessing a genuine miracle. There flies a dead duck!'"[9]

Confidence is the feeling or belief that you can do something well or succeed. Yet research shows few people are born confident. One study, from geneticist and psychologist Robert Plomin, makes an argument that some people may get a genetic boost toward confidence.[10] He researched 15,000 sets of twins in Britain, testing them in three academic subjects (math, writing, and science), then asking them to rate how confident they were about their abilities in each subject. He theorized that genetics have an impact on confidence (as defined by your perceived ability to do well) of up to 50 percent while the rest is affected by environment, experiences, and upbringing. Plomin's study clearly showed that believing you will succeed is a reliable predictor of actually doing so.

Truth is, the confident person _____ to be that way—and you can, too.

ELIZABETH'S STORY

Intelligent, spirited, and compassionate, Elizabeth stands up for her choices and beliefs. This was never more evident than in her decision to prioritize her marriage and her family over the legacy of her past. Elizabeth was raised in an environment that featured specific practices and traditions exclusive to her heritage, but she had the confidence to set those aside to embrace the new and different ideas and customs of her husband and friends.

In particular, Elizabeth's mother wasn't pleased by this, and she and others even conspired against Elizabeth's relationship with her husband—but Elizabeth steadfastly stood against those challenges and for her new family and their lifestyle. She also possesses a great sense of humor which she often uses to lighten the mood during a stressful situation. She often makes people laugh with her unique signature reaction to the unexpected of "Oh, my stars!" She also once told her mother, "You know, this has been the strangest morning. First, my husband starts asking ridiculous questions, and then you pop in like Lady Macbeth doing the neglected mother bit."

In the end, Elizabeth's kind nature and bravery have combined to allow her to retain a relationship with her mother and others from her past while she continues to build and embrace what she feels is a truly magical present and future with her family. It's all because she has learned to be confident, and she works to stay that way.

Questions for application:

1. Name one way you have evolved from the person you were in the past to think and live differently today?

    _____

    _____

    _____

    _____

    _____

2. How does that continue to give you confidence to handle daily challenges?

    _____

    _____

    _____

    _____

    _____

3. List a current stressful situation, then speculate on how you can use humor to lighten the mood as you deal with it.

_____

_____

_____

_____

_____

Confidence killers

Confidence is a cornerstone of leadership. It is also the incubator for the embryo of your dreams and the birthplace of your destiny. But in order to learn and develop the triumphant confidence you desire, you will need to confront and overcome three confidence killers.

Killer 1: Low self-esteem.

The self-defeating thought, "I don't think I can," rises from a deeper, more destructive belief that says, "I don't think I _am_." This causes you to more easily give up _____ to get what you want.

I understand how paralyzing low self-esteem can be. Early in my time at General Motors, I was made the lead project engineer of the rack and pinion steering gear line, taking over for a gentleman who had been there four times as long as I had. The cost, responsibility, and overall care of this line was critically important to the well-being of the entire plant. To say that I was nervous is an understatement, but I had to find the confidence deep within to meet the responsibility given to me. I spoke self-assuring words to myself, focusing on positive outcomes for the production line. Whenever doubts arose, I put my mind on achieving high results. Above average was the minimum I would accept.

It turned out that I remained in that position for the next five years. The line was very successful, and I ended up being promoted to another plant to take over a half shaft line as project manager.

1. Right now, speak three self-assuring words to yourself. Write them down here.

_____

_____

_____

2. Briefly describe how each word infused your confidence.

_____

_____

_____

_____

_____

Killer 2: Fear.

I believe it was the great motivational speaker, author, and sales expert Zig Ziglar who popularized the compelling acronym for fear as being False Evidence Appearing Real—and I have found that acronym to be undeniably true.

I can trace two specific fears back to my childhood: the fear of loud noises and the fear of falling. One day when I was seven, I was visiting my granddad, and a fire truck zoomed by with its siren wailing as I was playing outside. For some reason, I thought the engine was trying to get me—and I scrambled so fast to run away from it that I hit my head on the brick corner of the apartment building. I had to get stitches, and I still bear the scar from the injury. I told my mother what happened, and about three months later, she took me to visit someone she knew who worked at a fire station. He took us inside, got up in the fire truck, and turned on the siren. I was afraid at first and felt like running away once more. But after a few moments, I realized the truck was not trying to get me. The fire engine wasn't a bad thing at all.

My fear of falling came from dreams I had as a child. In them, I always fell off a high cliff. I could see and feel myself plummeting toward the earth, but I would never reach it. I just kept helplessly tumbling through the air. I overcame this fear by imagining myself landing safely on my feet as if I were Superman coming in for a landing.

DICK'S STORY

If Dick fears one thing above anything else, it is the unknown. A confident account executive at a marketing firm, Dick thrives on knowing the details of every campaign from strategy to visual design. He feels in control at work. But whenever his wife, a clever and creative personality, wants to use her more unconventional means to solve their problems, it makes Dick uncomfortable. He often tries to stop her, preferring his more comfortable solutions to hers.

However, Dick has learned to overcome this fear as he observes his wife handling the challenges put before them using her effective, albeit unusual, methodologies. He's discovered that letting go of his desire to control every little thing that happens has not only increased his trust and confidence in his wife, but it's bolstered his own self-confidence as he experiences the benefits of sharing the load of life. He's also found that his wife's consistent respect for him and his felt need to feel in control has caused him to respect her more in return, deepening their relationship and love for one another.

Defeating his fear of the unknown has made Dick more confident in the present and better equipped for his future personally and professionally.

Questions for application:

1. What is your greatest fear?

_____

_____

_____

_____

_____

2. How does it impact your professional life?

_____

_____

_____

_____

_____

3. How does it manifest itself in your personal life?

_____

_____

_____

_____

I have discovered five practical ways you can conquer your fears.

1. Practice reacting aggressively and positively toward the fears in your imagination: As you do this, it will be just a matter of time before those mental reactions extend into your physical world and become a reality in your actual life. As soon as you identify a negative thought creeping into your mind, _____ your internal dialogue to reverse the thought and put a positive spin to it. Replace irrational "what ifs" with "I'll handle it," "It can be done," or "I'll figure it out."

    How can you react aggressively and positively to your greatest fear?

    _____

    _____

    _____

    _____

    _____

2. Change the atmosphere: Take risks, and set out to do what your heart desires. As Lee Ann Womack sang, "When you get the choice to sit it out or dance, I hope you dance." Despite my earlier success as a student, when I was at Kettering University, I possessed an abiding fear of taking tests. I was nervous and scared that I wouldn't do my best. I conquered this with a little role play. I dressed in a business suit and tie. I may have looked different than my classmates on test days, but in that attire, I felt like I was getting down to business. I'd sit down at my desk convinced that it was time to *take care* of business! The technique worked brilliantly.

    The single most important thing you can do to build self-confidence is to actually go out and _____ what you fear. Afraid to fly? Take a short flight with a trusted friend. Scared of heights? Go to the upper floor of a building and stay near the window for a spell. Claustrophobic? Take a favorite book or music with you, turn on the light, and sit in your closet. Safely but boldly face your fears.

    What can you do to face your greatest fear?

    _____

    _____

    _____

    _____

    _____

3. Act as if it is impossible to fail: When you know that it can be done, you can invoke the ability already within you that will enable you to do it. If a mistake happens along the way, don't dwell on it. Just _____ your actions as you go along.

How can you act as if it is impossible to fail and overcome your greatest fear?

_____

_____

_____

_____

_____

4. Relax your fear away: Psychological studies suggest that it is not possible for you to feel fear when the muscles of your body are perfectly relaxed. So, the moment you recognize that anxiety is creeping in and your muscles start to tighten up, focus on loosening them. _____ is an excellent tool to combat and conquer fear.

What can you do daily to relax your greatest fear away?

_____

_____

_____

_____

_____

5. Substitute the feeling of fear with another positive, "feel good" feeling: Think about anything that strikes a chord and leaves you with a pleasant sensation. Capture that feeling and use it to _____ your fear.

A good friend of mine was going in for an MRI and knew he'd feel uncomfortable being inside the tube of the machine. It made him feel trapped like a cork in a bottle. What did he do? During the entire 20 minute procedure, he closed his eyes and envisioned himself at a wide open baseball stadium watching a game with his grandchild, reliving a treasured memory of a past event and experiencing how it made him feel: happy and peaceful. He made it through the MRI without having to even think about hitting the panic button.

What "feel good" feeling can you employ to offset your greatest fear?

_____

_____

_____

_____

_____

Killer 3: Other people's opinions of you.

If you worry about what other people think of you, it is because you have placed more confidence in them and their _____ than in yourself.

When I first got started in motivational speaking and facilitating leadership trainings, I was criticized by a gentleman who was a leader and well-known speaker in the community. He told me point blank that I was not a good speaker because I did not enunciate my words properly and spoke too fast. At first, I entertained what he said—but I quickly realized that I had been given a special gift from God to engage and share with others.

I concluded that his opinion was just that, an opinion, which ultimately had no bearing on who I was and what I was striving to become.

1. List an opinion someone has recently shared about you.

_____

_____

_____

_____

_____

2. How can you use self-confidence to refute that opinion?

_____

_____

_____

_____

_____

Triumphant Attributes and Traits

Thursday is uniquely positioned in the work week. It's not quite Friday yet, but you can feel it, right? The conclusion of the week is near. Saturday and the weekend are not that far away. As much as Wednesday is the mid-week "hump" day, Thursday is that day when you feel you are starting to turn the corner toward the finish line.

There's an anticipation to Thursday that makes you want to do everything in your power to make it positive and, well, triumphant—and here are four great attributes, followed by four key traits, that make that possible.

1. **It's a day to begin with the end in mind.**

    Thursday is a perfect day to know what you want to accomplish from the very beginning. That way, everything else you do can _____ you to where you want to go.

    One summer, my staff and I at Ability Plus were dealing with a daunting challenge to finalize our detailed policies and procedures in order to accommodate new government guidelines for our organization. One specific Thursday, I woke up with extra anticipation that we were going to accomplish our assignment. I was determined to see the end of the exercise fulfilled, and the sunny, beautiful morning fed my optimism. I knew the day was going to be long and tedious with a lot of work ahead, but I saw the finish line. That day ended up being pivotal to us completing the policies and procedures. Shortly after that, we were able to put the final period on the last sentence of the project.

AGNES' STORY

Agnes never went a single day without the end in mind during her lifelong career as a performer. She began performing as a child and sang on local radio programs when she was older. She continued to write and perform as she attended three different colleges, earning a Ph.D. in literature. She even taught high school for a few years while attending the American Academy of Performing Arts. But it was Agnes' breakthrough with Orson Welles' famed Mercury Theatre troupe that brought her acclaim and further opportunities.

From then on, one thing led to another, and a variety of film and television roles followed to take Agnes where she wanted to go and beyond. She kept working until two years before her death, her career and life full of achievement and purpose.

"I am a self-disciplined person," she said, "and my Bible is my security, guiding me in that discipline. I'm a woman of strong convictions." Regarding her confident motivation, Agnes added, "I always consider what I am doing at the moment the finest thing in my life. I find there's more happiness that way than in forever taking old triumphs out of trunks and dusting them off."

Questions for application:

1. Agnes cited her self-discipline, faith, and conviction as sources for her daily drive to succeed. What one thing compels you forward each day?

   _____

2. How can you use that to help you do a better job living each day with the end in mind?

   _____
   _____
   _____
   _____
   _____

3. Think about your goals for tomorrow—and determine what you need to do first thing in the morning to position yourself to meet them.

   _____
   _____
   _____
   _____
   _____

2. **It's a day to put your thoughts in their place.**

   If you place your hand over an open flame, your brain responds so that you won't do that again. But that survival mechanism can also work against you because it causes you to focus on the negative rather than the positive. Therefore, you want to train your brain to _____ the good over the bad in whatever situations you face. Here are some simple yet profound ways you can do just that.

   Forget each kindness that you do as soon as you have done it.
   Forget the praise that falls to you the moment you have won it.
   Forget the slander that you hear before you can repeat it.
   Forget each slight, each spite, each sneer, whenever you may meet it.

Remember every promise made and keep it to the letter.
Remember those who lend you aid and be a grateful debtor.
Remember all the happiness that comes your way in living.
Forget each worry and distress; be hopeful and forgiving.
Remember good, remember truth, remember to love those around you.
And you will find, through age and youth, that many will love you, too.[11]

Which one of these thoughts do you most resonate with right now—and why?

_____

_____

_____

_____

_____

3. It's a day to take control of self-talk.

How often do you speak powerful, positional words to yourself? Like the prize fighter who looks in the mirror and declares himself to be a champion before entering the ring, you should _____ yourself to excel and win!

I was scheduled to do the keynote address at the NAVIGATE Nonprofit Network Conference 2022 in Huntsville, Alabama. The premier conference in the region for nonprofit leaders, boards, and their supporters with over 600 participants, my address took place on a Thursday. Before heading to the stage, I looked in a mirror. "You got this!" I told myself. "Go out there and 'Doc Rock 'Em!'" The keynote went wonderfully, I had a great time, and even the mayor of the city was excited by my presentation.

Remember your biggest challenge from earlier this week. Now, pretend you are looking in the mirror. What would you say to yourself to ignite your confidence to be triumphant?

_____

_____

_____

_____

_____

4. **It's a day to expand beyond your comfort zone.**

When you intentionally step outside your comfort zone, it expands. If we stay within it, that zone eventually starts to shrink. You will avoid this by _____ yourself to do things that stretch you and even involve some risk.

When I was a young engineer, I wasn't very comfortable speaking to executives about a project. So, when several executives came from headquarters to look at new projects and processes that we had been working on at the Saginaw division of General Motors, I was quite nervous and did everything I could to get out of the presentation. I thought my manager, or another teammate, could do it for me. But instead of running from the situation and my responsibility, I mustered up the courage to push myself to give the presentation anyway. My managers and others were very satisfied with it, giving me a new sense of confidence that I had never experienced before and that still carries over today.

MARION'S STORY

She couldn't help herself. Between her endearing personality and eccentric tendencies—she was an avid collector of doorknobs, for example—Marion was her family's favorite aunt. But as she aged, not only did she start having normal struggles with her memory (She kidded, "I know I'm a little vague at times, but on the other hand, when I forget something, I'm definite."), Marion began seeking purpose beyond what she had always been. She wanted her later years to have new meaning.

Marion found that meaning when she went outside of her comfort zone and began babysitting elementary school-aged children. Nervous that she wouldn't be good at childcare after so many decades apart from her own child-rearing years, Marion didn't even want to try it at first. But with the encouragement of a beloved niece, not only has Marion discovered she is still proficient at taking care of kids, but the children under her charge love her campy wit and zany stories. Even her doorknob collection has found new admirers in the boys and girls she cares for.

As she pushed herself to do something that stretched her and even made her feel a bit at risk, Marion discovered a purpose that has informed her elder years and even provided some welcome part-time income. She enjoys the children she babysits, and they appreciate her as if she was their own aunt.

Questions for application:

1. Describe a time in the past year when you stepped outside of your comfort zone.

_____

_____

_____

_____

_____

2. How did that experience expand your life?

_____

_____

_____

_____

_____

3. Marion broke out of her comfort zone in her older years. What does her story say to you about the rewards of stretching yourself and taking risks at your current age?

_____

_____

_____

_____

_____

The four common traits of the person who makes Thursdays triumphant emphasize a willingness to seek assistance and to have resilience.

Trait 1. Ask for help.

A three-year-old girl was getting ready to head upstairs to get ready for bed when she asked her father to come with her to help.

"You know how to undress yourself," her dad gently reminded her.

"Yes," she explained, "but sometimes people need people anyway, even if they know how to do things themselves."

Smiling, the dad followed his girl up to her room, thankful for the lesson on helpfulness she had given him.[12] The child didn't assume her father knew what she wanted. She made her request for help, and her reason for wanting it, clear.

It may be for their expertise or just their presence—but be ready to let other people know what you want—because once they _____ you want their help, you will be surprised at how forthcoming and appreciative they are to provide it.

Who do you need to ask for help today? What do you hope they can do for you?

_____

_____

_____

_____

_____

Trait 2. Find a mentor.

Whatever you've set out to do, there are likely others who've done it first and can offer you useful advice or serve as a role model. Find those people and _____ as much as you can from them.

The greatest mentor in my life was Dr. Maurice K. Wright. When I was starting my assignment as CEO of Ability Plus, he offered me wisdom that gave me both leadership direction and stability. I had an issue with a group of individuals who were trying to hurt me and the company. They not only harshly criticized what we were doing, but they claimed that we were lying about our processes and that they were not up to state standards. It made me angry, and I really wanted to retaliate and go after them.

Yet there's a reason I say that everyone needs a "Dr. Wright!" He mentored me through the ordeal, meeting with me on a weekly basis. He identified my blind spots, such as letting my emotions take over. He pointed out that if I kept being good, moving forward, and doing the right things, I would prevail. With Dr. Wright's counsel, direction, and patience, both me and the company came to a positive outcome from the situation.

1. If you have had, or currently have, a mentor, describe how that person has benefitted you the most.

_____

_____

_____

_____

_____

2. If you have never had a mentor, list how finding a mentor could help you and why.

_____

_____

_____

_____

_____

Trait 3. Get ready to bounce back.

It's not failure that destroys your confidence, it's not getting back up. Failure is an _____ in the process of success. Once you get back up, you've learned what doesn't work and can give it another try. Don't allow anything to keep you from reaching your desired destination.

Everybody recognizes that Ludwig van Beethoven was a musical genius. But few realize the adversity he had to overcome to achieve greatness. In his twenties, Beethoven began to lose his hearing. The problem haunted him into the middle years of his life, but he kept it a guarded secret. By the time he reached his fifties, Beethoven was completely deaf. But he refused to give up. He was once overheard shouting at the top of his voice, "I will take life by the throat!" Many of his biographers believe the only reason Beethoven remained productive for so long was his undaunted determination to bounce back.[13]

What is something you need to "get back up" from today? What do you think you will learn as you do?

_____

_____

_____

_____

Trait 4. Choose your companions wisely.

Your general outlook, negative or positive, will reflect the cumulative average perspective of the five people you spend the most time with—so make sure you're hanging out with people who encourage you and lift you up. The opinions of others matter and speak to your _____, which will impact your confidence.

In my book *God-A-Tude* published in 2021, I mentioned an old saying of mine: "I don't hang with chickens. I eat chicken, but I hang with eagles." I have a group of leaders in my life—men and women who own companies, build people, and show care for society— and I call them "eagles." Each one of these five people have shown me how to keep fighting and to win. One of them once challenged me to do better during a staff meeting by asking me to look at financial data a little deeper and trim some things to reduce the budget and improve overall stewardship of our funds.

It was tough. I wasn't expecting it, and it upset me at first. Yet he told me, "If you keep questioning your decisions, you'll never be great." He challenged me to never accept average and to have the confidence that I could do whatever I worked to do. I accepted his direction, reworked the budget, and everyone was better for it.

ALICE'S STORY

Ever had a nosy neighbor? Alice did. Sandra lived across the street with her husband, Pierce, and she became the bane of Alice's life. She'd catch Sandra frequently peeking at her through the curtains of her home, and every time Sandra stopped by, she questioned Alice, convinced that something strange was going on with her or her family. Sandra was irrepressible.

For a while, Alice tolerated Sandra's interrogations. Then they started making her angry, and it was everything Alice could do not to tell Sandra off. Finally, after another unexpected visit and confrontation, Alice decided to go over to Sandra's house herself and have it out. When she arrived, though, Alice looked around and noticed that Sandra lived a pretty spartan lifestyle. She didn't have much, and she could sense that her husband generally didn't want to have much to do with his oft-nagging wife. Suddenly and quite unexpectedly, Alice felt compassion for her nosy neighbor.

"Would you like to get together for coffee once a week, over at my house?" Alice offered. "I think it would be best if we got to know one another better."

Sandra's usual blank gaze and confused exasperation gave way to a smile. It transformed her face. "Thank you," she replied. "I would like that very much."

Admittedly, Alice knew her invitation would appeal to Sandra's nosy nature—but as their weekly coffee visits got underway, Sandra not only discovered that there was nothing to be nosy about when it came to Alice, but there were things about Alice's demeanor and friendship that she desperately needed. As Alice spoke to Sandra's feelings, she started becoming more confident in herself. That decreased her suspiciousness and improved her behavior toward Alice, her husband, and herself.

Questions for application:

1. Sandra chose her companions, like Alice, by being meddlesome and intrusive. What could she have done better to develop friendships in her life?

_____

_____

_____

_____

_____

2. Alice decided to choose Sandra as a companion when she saw her neighbor's negative daily existence. How do you think Alice benefitted from nurturing a friendship with Sandra?

_____

_____

_____

_____

_____

3. Briefly list the five people you spend the most time with—and then write down the one thing they do best to positively impact your confidence, and why that helps you.

_____

_____

_____

_____

_____

Defining principles

The fourth day of the workweek can have its downside, though. As much as it is a day for anticipation, it can also be a day that easily gives way to apathy. Perhaps you're feeling weary and can't wait for the week to end and the weekend to arrive. You can let down your guard and decrease your effort and focus.

Here is a trio of preparation principles that, when you allow them to define your Triumphant Thursday, will keep such indifference at bay.

Do your homework.

Preparation will help boost your confidence. Have to give a speech? Practice it several times, record yourself, and listen. Meeting people for the first time? Learn more about them and their organizations in advance. Facing a challenging assignment? Do your _____.

Several centuries ago, a Japanese emperor commissioned an artist to paint a bird. A number of months passed, but still no painting was brought to the palace. Finally, the emperor became so exasperated that he went to the artist's home to demand an explanation.

Instead of making excuses, the artist placed a blank canvas on the easel. In less than an hour, he completed the painting that went on to become a brilliant masterpiece. When the emperor asked the reason for the delay, the artist showed him armloads of drawings of feathers, wings, heads, and feet. Then he explained that all of that research and study was necessary before he could begin and complete the painting.[14]

List a challenging assignment that is ahead on your schedule. What can you do now to better prepare for it in advance?

_____

_____

_____

_____

_____

Get plenty of rest and exercise.

There's ample evidence that sleep, exercise, and good nutrition profoundly affects both your mood and your effectiveness. Moderate exercise just three times a week for 20 minutes each time does much to fight depression and maintain a _____ attitude of success and confidence.

Once I began coaching and consulting, I decided that if I was going to teach others to be disciplined and to reach their dreams, I had to be disciplined with my own physical fitness. Each morning, I began exercising for at least 15 minutes. That eventually developed into a daily 30-minute regimen of push-ups, sit ups, squats, leg kicks, and dumbbell work. I don't go to a gym. I have an area in my home office for these activities—an area where I have a big fabric banner someone gave to me that declares, "No Bad Days!" I've found it is very refreshing to accomplish a physical feat early in the morning. It's a way that I say to each day, "Let's go!"

1. How often and for how long do you exercise each week?

_____

_____

2. On average, how much do you restfully sleep every night?

_____

3. What can you do now to increase the amount and improve the quality of both?

_____

_____

_____

_____

_____

Align your intention with your impact.

I came across a story about two men who went hunting. Neither one was a terribly good shot, so after they had tramped through the fields for hours, they had yet to hit anything. With evening coming on, both were getting tired. One turned to the other and said, "What about it? Let's just miss two more and call it a day." Despite the lack of anything to show for their time, the two hunters probably expended as much energy and effort as if they had been successful.

The same thing can happen to you. "It is not enough to be busy," someone once said. "One must also get results."[15] Figure out the impact that you want to make in a given situation and _____ your intentions with the results of that impact. Be intentional in all that you do!

1. List a specific personal or professional goal, then write down the primary outcome (impact) you desire from meeting that goal.

_____

_____

_____

_____

_____

2. What are three objectives (intentions) you need to achieve to realize that impact?

_____

_____

_____

3. Give each objective a deadline—and go after it!

_____

_____

_____

_____

_____

_____

A pompous young man once came to the great philosopher, Socrates, asking for knowledge. Socrates recognized the type of person he was dealing with and led the young man through the streets, to the sea, and then chest deep into the water. "What do you want?" Socrates asked.

"Knowledge, O wise Socrates," said the young man with a proud smile.

Socrates put his strong hands on the man's shoulders—and promptly pushed him under water. Thirty seconds later, Socrates let him up. "What do you want?" he asked again.

"Knowledge," the young man gasped.

Socrates sent him under again. Thirty more seconds passed before Socrates pulled the young man's head above the waves.

"What do you want, young man?"

Between heavy, heaving breaths, the humbled fellow wheezed. "Air!" he screeched. "I need air!"

Socrates put a supporting arm around the man. "When you want knowledge as much as you just wanted air, then you will have it."[16]

Socrates knew that the young man needed to have the appropriate _enthusiasm_ about what he wanted, above all else, in order to have the _drive_ to go after it and get it—and so do you. That's why I've made enthusiasm and drive the keynote of a Fantastic Friday!

Triumphant Thursday – Confidence **Fill-in-the-Blank Answer Key:**

unwavering	replace	learn
learns	opinions	ingredient
trying	lead	feelings
change	emphasize	research
do	motivate	positive
correct	pushing	align
Meditation	know	

Notes

6

FANTASTIC FRIDAY
Enthusiasm and Drive

I first discovered that I possessed drive when I was in engineering school at Kettering University. At the end of my freshman year, I was struggling. I felt out of place. I was away from my home in Alabama. I had no friends or family in Michigan. I began lacking confidence, and my grades were suffering accordingly. I was just about ready to give up.

That's when another treasured mentor, Dr. David Green, Jr., challenged me to fight for the goal of graduating. After his first talk with me, I developed an urge that morphed into an overwhelming desire to walk across that Kettering stage with my engineering degree in hand. I regularly envisioned the moment, and even attended graduation ceremonies that semester to motivate me further.

In May 1993, I not only lived out my vision, but I graduated with top grades and the honor of outstanding thesis. It was a major accomplishment. Even today, completing engineering school was the hardest thing I've ever done, greater than my master's degrees or earning my doctorate.

Dr. Green ignited my drive to achieve more than what I could see, feel, or even do on my own. He drilled me to believe in the gifts and talents God had given me. I'll never forget what he told me as he mentored me: "You can't regain lost time."

That statement changed my life. It made me look at time as my most important _____, realizing that I only have so much of it allocated to me and that I need to make the most of it with enthusiasm and drive. I have been very productive since then, and now I am leading three different organizations because I don't waste time.

Tell the story from your life that first came to mind when you read Dr. Green's words, "You can't regain lost time."

_____

_____

_____

_____

_____

Psychologists identify drive as an innate, determined urge to attain a goal or satisfy a need. It creates an insatiable _____ to become what you desire to be. The key ingredient to supporting and sustaining such drive in your life is enthusiasm. Defined as an intense and eager enjoyment, interest, or approval, enthusiasm creates a strong feeling of excitement about something that results in an absorbing, controlling _____ of your mind by that interest. Enthusiasm causes eagerness, energy, zeal, and gusto.

My sophomore year at Kettering was a turning point in my life—thanks to discovering my enthusiasm. It was two weeks into the first semester that I was elected president of the Black Unity Congress. As you read earlier, it took considerable time and effort for me to convince the BUC to get behind my vision to no longer be a segregated organization. The school was less than five percent African American, so we had to become more inclusive to drive up membership and increase our impact in assisting and mentoring students.

As I took on that challenge, I got so excited to lead the way. Enthusiasm welled up within me, infusing me to be a true, selfless servant leader. It was not about me. It was all about the cause of serving and helping others. We got more involved with the student body, developed a mentorship program with area churches, and sat in on the school's President's Council for the first time. Our funding surged. Being a servant leader became a controlling possession that still absorbs me today.

What is a controlling, absorbing possession in your life right now? Describe it, and explain why you are driven and enthusiastic about it.

_____

_____

_____

_____

Enthusiasm that fuels your drive can make all the difference on Friday when the long workweek is nearing its end, the weekend beckons, and you need that final push to not only get to the finish line, but to cross it ahead of the pack.

PATRICK'S STORY

As a leader, Patrick was both remarkably analytical and insatiably curious, two seemingly opposite qualities that he consistently combined to succeed at whatever enterprise he was given charge of. At the same time, Patrick's love of archaeology and literature (he often quoted Shakespeare to bring context to a given situation) seasoned his interests away from work.

However, Patrick rarely took time off from the job to relax and recharge. Several years ago, members of his leadership team and his physician convinced him to go on an extended holiday at a paradise resort. Gamefully, Patrick tried to rest, determined to lounge in the sun and catch up on his reading. He particularly enjoyed detective yarns. But a fellow vacationer lured him away, and they ended up spending the majority of his time off searching for a rare archaeological artifact. Patrick didn't rest much at all.

But he learned something invaluable. The adventure showed Patrick that he could channel the same enthusiasm and drive that made him a great leader into his recreational activities. Not only did Patrick relax, but he returned to work recharged and reenergized for service. It also made him more appreciative of his life in general. "Someone once told me that time is a predator that stalks us all our lives," he recently said. "But I rather believe that time is a companion that goes with us on a journey and reminds us to cherish every moment…because it will never come again."

Questions for application:

1. Do your enthusiasm and drive manifest themselves more when you're at work or at play? In what ways?

_____

_____

_____

_____

_____

2. How can you channel your enthusiasm and drive to help you in the area where it is least present?

_____

_____

_____

_____

3. Describe one way you can better "cherish every moment" in your professional or personal life.

_____

_____

_____

_____

Five attributes of a Fantastic Friday

Enthusiasm and drive will be your end-of-the-week companions as you allow this quintet of attributes to direct your attitude and your actions.

1. **I'm fired up to be a part!** When you can see yourself as being essential to doing something worthwhile, it gets you _____.

    When Rosina Hernandez was in college, she attended a rock concert at which one young man was brutally beaten by another. No one made an attempt to stop the beating. The next day, she was struck dumb to learn that the youth had died as a result of the pounding. Yet neither she, nor anyone else, had raised a hand to help him.

    She could never forget the incident or her responsibility as an inactive bystander.

    Some years later, Rosina saw another catastrophe. A car driving in the rain ahead of her suddenly skidded and plunged into a bay. The car landed head down in the water with only the tail end showing. In a moment, a woman appeared on the surface, shouting for help and saying her husband was stuck inside.

    This time Rosina waited for no one. She plunged into the water, tried unsuccessfully to open the car door, then pounded on the back window as other bystanders stood on the causeway and watched. First, she screamed at them, begging for help, then cursed them, telling them there was a man dying in the car.

First one man, then another, finally dived into the water to assist Rosina. Together, they broke the safety glass and dragged the man out. They were just in time. A few minutes later it would have been all over.

The woman thanked Rosina for saving her husband, and Rosina was elated, riding an emotional high that lasted for weeks. She had promised herself that she would never again fail to do anything she could to save a human life—and she had made good on her promise.[17]

What project for your family or initiative at work can you become so fired up about that you'll stop at nothing to see it through? Why?

_____

_____

_____

_____

2. **Go knock it out!** Sometimes, just getting something done is its own _____. My son, Joshua, encouraged us to upgrade to a programmable lighting system at our church. That required installing three new trusses in the ceiling and over 30 new lights on the trio of trusses. It was no small undertaking, and he wanted me to help. I looked at it as an opportunity to spend time with my incredibly smart and managerial son. We worked several days into the midnight hours to complete the task, but after it was finished, I felt such an incredible feeling. Together, my son and I had knocked it out!

Describe the last time you felt the satisfying reward of getting something done.

_____

_____

_____

_____

3. **It's great to be a part of this movement!** History is filled with movements that made a world-changing difference for communities, nations, and humankind. In the United States alone, five come to mind.

   The Boston Tea Party of 1773 was the first significant act of independence by American colonists against the British. The Women's Suffrage Parade in Washington D.C. in March 1913 took place on the eve of President Woodrow Wilson's inauguration and sparked other movements that finally led to the nineteenth amendment, which granted women the right to vote in 1920. The March on Washington for Jobs and Freedom in 1963 brought us Dr. Martin Luther King's iconic "I Have a Dream" speech and spurred the civil rights movement. The Stonewall Protests of 1969 propelled the LGBTQ+ community forward, and the Occupation of Alcatraz from 1969-1971 led to a new national policy of self-determination for Native Americans.

   Movements can lead to positive and sweeping _____, so why not view your key personal and professional goals the same way? What is happening in your life that can make a difference both now and in the future?

MARINA'S STORY

Gifted with a capability for extra-heightened empathy, Marina could often tell when others were anxious, afraid, or hiding something. As a teenager, this sensitivity seemed to be more of a curse than a blessing as she dealt with more than her fair share of drama from her friends and classmates. Marina also regularly butted heads with her eccentric, strong-willed mother. Still, she realized that she had an ability that would help others, if she could find a way to use it without compromising her own emotional well-being.

Marina found that when she went to college and pursued a major in psychology and a minor in life coaching. Studying both disciplines enabled her to harness her natural abilities through a grid of techniques and boundaries that allowed her to encourage and support others through their traumas while protecting her own heart and mind.

Today, Marina is a therapist who knows she is making a profound difference in the lives of her clients. With the steady increase of mental and emotional maladies affecting people in moden society, Marina believes she is an integral part of a curative movement that will better the human condition now and in the future. "We deal with our pain in many different ways," she said. "But over the years, I've discovered it's in joy that the uniqueness of each individual is revealed."

Questions for application:

1. What current personal or professional goal can you reimagine in the context of being part of a greater movement? How?

_____

_____

_____

_____

_____

2. What is a natural tendency of yours that could be directed toward a greater purpose? How?

_____

_____

_____

_____

3. How can you use joy to empower your enthusiasm and drive

_____

_____

_____

_____

4. **This is an incredible opportunity!** Opportunity is defined as a set of circumstances that make it _____ to do something that's never been done before, even out of tragedy. The Irish Potato Famine (1846-1851) resulted in a 30 percent drop in the population of western Ireland. The prolonged suffering of the Irish peasantry broke survivors in both body and spirit.

John Bloomfield, the owner of Castle Caldwell in County Fermanagh, was working on the recovery of his estate when he noticed that the exteriors of his tenant farmers' small cottages had a vivid white finish. He was informed that there was a clay deposit on his property of unusually fine quality. To generate revenue and provide employment on his estate, he built a pottery in the village of Belleek in 1857. The unusually fine clay yielded a porcelain china that was translucent with a glass-like finish.

It was worked into traditional Irish designs and was an immediate success. Belleek's iridescent pearlized glaze has been enthusiastically purchased the world over.[18] A multimillion-dollar industry rose from innovative thinking during some very troubling times.

What amazing opportunities await you at home or at work? List three.

1. _____

   _____

2. _____

   _____

3. _____

   _____

5. **This moment is huge!** You've surely heard the exhortation, "Be in the moment!" But how often are we actually there and ready to _____? When I was 16, I went to work as a lifeguard after completing six weeks of grueling, intense training that tested my mental, emotional, and physical discipline. As I began my first shift at the deepest end of the pool, I climbed up the ladder to take my seat—and saw through the water the wavering image of a little boy at the bottom of the pool. "Save him!" someone yelled.

I had trained precisely for that moment! My heart rate shot up and normal protocol went out the door. I was supposed to have blown my whistle three short times before acting. Instead, I dove into the water with my shirt on and my whistle still around my neck. Then I swam to the bottom, and brought the boy to the surface, placing him beside the pool. He was breathing and very scared, and I instantly let him know that he was safe before carrying him to a vending area for food and water. The moment was as huge as it gets, and my heart was just as large with joy!

1. Share the story of a similarly huge moment in your life.

    _____

    _____

    _____

    _____

    _____

2. Describe what it did to feed your enthusiasm and drive.

    _____

    _____

    _____

    _____

    _____

A difference maker

There is nothing more inspiring to your enthusiasm and drive than knowing that you are making a difference in the lives of those around you—especially on a Friday. These four characteristics will help you do just that.

Impart confidence to other people.

In his book, *The Quest for Character*, Charles Swindoll told the story of when Dr. Daniel Boorstin of the Library of Congress spoke of five items that were in President Abraham Lincoln's pockets the night he was assassinated in April of 1865. Included were several old and worn newspaper articles. "The clippings," said Boorstin, "were concerned with the great deeds of Abraham Lincoln. One of them actually reports a speech by John Bright which says that Abraham Lincoln is 'one of the greatest men of all times.'"

The world now knows that Bright, a British statesman, was correct in his assessment of Lincoln, but in 1865, millions of people shared quite a different opinion. Lincoln's critics were fierce and many, even as the president agonized over the suffering and turmoil of his country being ripped to shreds by hatred and Civil War. There is something touchingly poignant about the thought of this great leader seeking confidence and self-assurance from a few old newspaper clippings.[19]

Everyone needs confidence. Who can you impart confidence to today? How?

_____

_____

_____

_____

_____

Infuse hope in others.

In the late 1990s, I had the opportunity to infuse hope into a great guy. Keith was my classmate in high school, and he had fallen into a severe drug addiction. Late one evening, his sister asked me to go to the home of a friend he was staying with to encourage him not to give up on his life. I went and stood with Keith under the stars in the backyard, listening as he told me his story. It was one filled with hurt and disappointment.

My heart filled with compassion, and I began to paint a picture of what his future could look like if he made the decision to change his life. "Are you ready to change?" I asked.

I will never forget the look of expectation in Keith's eyes as he responded, "Yes, I am."

I knew he was serious, and I affirmed, "You are telling the truth."

Right there, Keith got down on his knees in the grass and repented to God. He later told me that my statement of confirmation gave him the confidence and drive he needed to move forward. Today, he runs a drug recovery program at our church and is doing great things.

DENISE'S STORY

Her childhood couldn't have been more tragic. Denise hardly remembers her parents, who were killed when she was just five years of age. She and her sister were temporarily taken in by friends until they were both turned over to the foster care system. There, the girls were separated and, for years, mistreated. Sexual and physical abuse became harsh realities for Denise as she bounced from one place to the next. By the time she was a young adolescent, Denise was afraid and filled with hurt and rage.

That's when Beth came into her life. A patient and caring foster mom, Beth helped Denise get therapy, and Beth nursed her through her past traumas. Eventually, Beth adopted Denise—and even though Denise was close to adult age by then, she welcomed being Beth's daughter. At the family ceremony recognizing the adoption, Denise told everyone, "You all know where I came from and what my life was like before, but Beth—my mom—took that frightened, angry young girl and tempered her."

Denise went into military service as an adult, and she has gone on to inspire countless men and women through her service and leadership. Denise used the pain and lessons learned from her past, and the love and redemption of her selfless mother, as enthusiasm and drive to bring hope to others. Denise is also on a search to find, and hopefully be reunited with, her sister.

Questions for application:

1. Both Keith and Denise overcame much to become what they are today. How do you believe redemption serves to foster enthusiasm and drive in someone?

_____

_____

_____

_____

_____

2. Like I did with Keith and Beth did for Denise, who can you intervene for to bring hope into their lives? Write their first name here.

_____

_____

_____

_____

_____

3. Briefly describe how you believe you can help them, and why.

_____

_____

_____

_____

_____

Keep pushing forward.

Sometimes we can get excited about a project but then have that enthusiasm _____ by unforeseen circumstances. Such was the case for me in 2002 when I was taking the lead to organize a Christian minister's conference. We planned for months in advance, calling potential speakers, getting volunteers, and marketing the event. Then, just one week before the conference, we had to move to a completely new venue because of a scheduling error for the original location.

Panic could've set in, but I knew that we had to keep calm, figure out a plan to relocate the conference, and get the word out to our speakers, volunteers, and attendees. We had to clean the new location's classrooms and rearrange several event activities there, but we pushed forward, allowing no excuses that we couldn't get it done. We pulled it off, and the conference turned out to be a great success.

1. What is usually your first response when unforeseen circumstances change your plans?

   _____

   _____

   _____

   _____

   _____

2. How can you change that response to keep your enthusiasm and drive in the future?

   _____

   _____

   _____

   _____

   _____

Recondition the mind to accept the creative thought "climate."

Climate, as most of us think of it, refers to the long-term pattern of weather in a particular area. Weather can change from day-to-day, month-to-month, or even year-to-year. A region's weather patterns, usually tracked for at least 30 years, are considered its climate.

Now think of your brain. The long-term pattern of your thoughts, decisions, and actions makes up the _____ of your life. A wise adage declares, "As a man thinks, so is he." How can you transform your thinking to stimulate the creativity and inventiveness you need to bring renewed enthusiasm and drive to your life? It'll likely start with dedicating more time for learning and personal development which takes you out of your comfort zone and stretches you mentally.

What can you do to encourage those around you to change the climate of their thinking to become more creative? Explain.

Parting principles to head into the weekend

Even in this day of flexible schedules that depart from the traditional workweek model, the cry of "TGIF!" remains. There's still just something about Friday that lets you know that a welcome reprieve is coming. These eight principles of a Fantastic Friday will help you enter into that time informed and energized.

1. **Enthusiasm is caught, not taught, through relationships:** I caught the enthusiasm I needed to start motivational speaking one evening during a financial conference at the Von Braun Center in Huntsville. It was there, inside a packed arena filled with 10,000 people, that I first saw and heard the great Zig Ziglar. He delivered a keynote called Living Your Dream about going forward and getting out of your comfort zone. It was electrifying, and his energy was so compelling that I was preoccupied for days afterward thinking of how I could motivate people to be their best. I left that event telling myself, "I can do that. I know I can! I've just got to work on some things to get there." I was ready to go and empower others to change the world!

How can you "TGIF!" your mindset at the close of each workweek to catch more enthusiasm and carry it into each weekend?

---

2. **Drive is the essential ingredient to success:** The late politician and educator Mark Hatfield told of touring Calcutta, India with Mother Teresa and visiting the places where sick children were cared for in their last days and the dispensary where the poor lined up by the hundreds to receive medical attention. As he watched Mother Teresa feeding and nursing those left behind by others, Hatfield was overwhelmed by the sheer magnitude of the suffering she and her co-workers faced daily. "How can you bear the load without being crushed by it?" he asked.

Mother Teresa replied, "My dear senator, I am not called to be successful. I am called to be faithful."[20]

Mother Teresa was driven by her calling, and her success was shown in how she helped others who were helpless. Allow whatever it is that drives you to _____ you to succeed both personally and professionally.

How can you "TGIF!" your mindset at the close of each workweek to have more drive and carry it into each weekend?

_____

_____

_____

_____

_____

3. **Without enthusiasm, we are scarcely willing to endure the self-discipline and endless toil that is necessary to develop professional skill:** When I started the 18-month program to earn my graduate certificate in business from Vanderbilt University, I was plenty enthusiastic about it—but I was promoted to chief operating officer of Ability Plus during that same time period. I knew that the program was going to be very beneficial to me, but it wasn't going to be easy, especially while maintaining my new professional responsibilities.

Therefore, I had to engage a higher level of self-discipline into my daily routine. About halfway through the program at Vanderbilt, one of the classes, Executive Leadership, was particularly demanding. It had more than the normal amount of homework and a special project as well. I knew I had no time to spare. It took some supreme discipline to keep up with it all, but I did it, and it was worth it. I'm still using the skills I developed during that program.

BRENT'S STORY

"His wonder, his curiosity about every facet of human nature, allowed all of us to see the best parts of ourselves. He evolved, and he embraced change because he always wanted to be better than he was."

That was the high praise and admiration given by a trusted friend about Brent, an operations management officer whose zeal toward self-improvement from better understanding those around him was unmatched in the corporation where he served. Brent tirelessly learned from his colleagues and sought to apply those lessons to how he worked and interacted with others. He refined his physical and mental capabilities to extraordinary levels. Brent's computational skills were off the charts. His ability to stay on task for long periods of time was remarkable.

Yet Brent wasn't at all a workaholic. He enjoyed painting and writing. His self-discipline became most useful (and tested) when he became the father of a daughter, Hallie, with his wife, Natasha. It also led him to make a career change so that he could dedicate more time to his family. When asked to explain why he lives the way he does, Brent was characteristically pragmatic. "It is true I am acting on my personal beliefs. But I do not see how I can do otherwise."

Questions for application:

1. What one task at work can you become more self-disciplined about? Explain.

_____

_____

_____

_____

_____

2. How can you best utilize your personal beliefs to improve your self-discipline?

_____

_____

_____

_____

_____

3. How can you "TGIF!" your mindset at the close of each workweek to infuse your self-discipline and carry it into each weekend?

_____

_____

_____

_____

_____

4. **Drive is the dynamic motivator that keeps us persistently working toward our goals:** In the spring of 1883, two young men graduated from medical school. They differed from one another in both appearance and ambition. Ben was short and stocky. Will was tall and thin. Ben dreamed of practicing medicine on the East Coast. Will wanted to work in a rural community. Ben begged his friend to go to New York with him, believing they could both make a fortune there, but Will refused.

His friend thought he was foolish for wanting to practice medicine in the Midwest. "But," Will insisted, "I want first of all to be a great surgeon, the very best, if I have the ability."

Years later, the wealthy and powerful came from around the world to be treated by Will at his clinic: the Mayo Clinic.[21] Will's foremost goal was not to pursue wealth, but to be great at what he did. That was the motivation that drove him—and his reward was more than he could've imagined. Let your drive propel you _____ what will make you truly great!

How can you "TGIF!" your mindset at the close of each workweek to improve your motivation and carry it into each weekend?

_____

_____

_____

_____

_____

5. **Enthusiasm informs our future:** During his 1960 presidential campaign, John F. Kennedy often closed his speeches with the story of Colonel Davenport, the former speaker of the Connecticut House of Representatives. Kennedy told of one day in 1789 when the skies over the city of Hartford darkened ominously, and some of the representatives, glancing out the windows, feared the end was at hand. Among the clamor, Davenport rose and said, "The Day of Judgment is either approaching

or it is not. If it is not, there is no cause for adjournment. If it is, I choose to be found doing my duty. Therefore, I wish that candles be brought."[22]

Rather than being afraid of what is to come, we are to be faithful to the job at hand. The future is not to be feared. It is to be enthusiastically embraced as the _____ that it is—for it is that very enthusiasm that affects and dictates how you face the days ahead.

How can you "TGIF!" your mindset at the close of each workweek to feel better about the future and carry it into each weekend?

_____

_____

_____

_____

_____

6. **Drive affects our outlook on life:** My drive to be the best I can be has been a constant positive _____ in my life—particularly when it comes to having influence in my community. I didn't pursue that influence to feel important or become popular. I did it to fulfill a calling on my life to help people reach their maximum potential.

Truth is, though, many people will not hear you or give any value to what you have to say if they feel you are not influential. So, I have successfully been appointed to several boards of influence in the community, allowing me to move the needle in several areas including education, health, and finance. Through my influence with these organizations, positive change has occurred with ethnic minorities being given greater opportunities to better help their businesses, contribute, and help others. It's gone beyond basic diversity and inclusion efforts, and we've seen tremendous results.

How can you "TGIF!" your mindset at the close of each workweek to have a more positive outlook and carry it into each weekend?

_____

_____

_____

_____

_____

7. **Enthusiasm affects our influence on others to progress:** When musician Pablo Casals reached the age of 95, a young reporter asked him a question. "Mr. Casals, you are the greatest cellist that ever lived. Why do you still practice six hours a day?"

Casals' answer: "Because I think I'm making progress."[23]

Truly great people never think they're great enough. They are always enthusiastic to progress and improve. Can you imagine the impact Casals had on young musicians as they watched the elder genius practice his craft? What about the impact you can have on others as you influence them to become more than they are right now?

JONATHAN'S STORY

Whether it's as a business leader, a chef, or a jazz musician, Jonathan's passion and enthusiasm is contagious. Though he can come across as arrogant and even brusque to some, it's evident that his self-confidence energizes everything he does, allowing him to engage others with gusto.

But beneath all that is the mind and heart of a learner. Through much trial and some error along the way, Jonathan has come to recognize areas of needed improvement as well as strengths he can leverage. That has birthed a growing sense of humility within him that has endeared him to his colleagues and enabled Jonathan to become more influential with them. He is a trusted mentor even as he continues to receive regular mentorship. An example of Jonathan's ability to influence others came when he told one mentee, "One of your strengths is your ability to evaluate the dynamics of a situation and then take a definitive, pre-emptive step, take charge. Now you're frustrated because you not only can't see a solution, but you can't define the problem." Such insights fueled his interactions.

No wonder Jonathan believes it's the greatest challenges that yield the best rewards. "The more difficult the task," he says, "the sweeter the victory."

Questions for application:

1. It often takes difficulty to cause us to move toward our own greatness. Briefly describe a challenge you faced this past month.

_____

_____

_____

_____

_____

2. How were you able to positively influence others as you faced that situation?

_____

_____

_____

_____

_____

3. How can you "TGIF!" your mindset at the close of each workweek to be more influential toward others and carry it into each weekend?

_____

_____

_____

_____

_____

8. **Drive affects our commitment:** There's a saying I've heard that I absolutely love, even if it is grammatically incorrect. "To succeed in life, you need not only initiative, but also finishiative."[24] We need to have the _____ of a finisher!

    One year I oversaw a kid's summer camp project at my church, and I had the vision and drive to make it the best summer camp in the entire Huntsville area. We did not want to exclude anyone. Yet we hit one roadblock after another. Sponsors bailed out. Volunteers were not able to keep or complete their commitments. We wouldn't be deterred. We even did a special program where kids participated in building an actual go-kart that looked like a little Hummer. One of our elders was a mechanic who was very creative, and he led the charge.

    The camp was an amazing success. The smiles from the kids were everything to us! When we took everyone to the Civil Rights Museum in Birmingham, Alabama, one of the children had never been outside our area or to the big city. It blew him away, and it expanded what he felt like he could do in life.

How can you "TGIF!" your mindset at the close of each workweek to have increased "finishiative" and carry it into each weekend?

_____

_____

_____

_____

_____

It's been quite a journey so far, hasn't it? From Sunday through Friday, we've learned how vision, attitude, belief, potential, confidence, and now enthusiasm and drive can feed one off the other and combine to send you soaring through your week with *No Bad Days*. But where does it all lead? To a Successful Saturday, of course, and the final element you need: purpose.

Fantastic Friday – Enthusiasm and Drive **Fill-in-the-Blank Answer Key:**

commodity	change	empower
appetite	possible	toward
possession	respond	opportunity
going	challenged	force
reward	climate	mindset

7

SUCCESSFUL SATURDAY
Purpose

Dr. Martin Luther King, Jr. surely said it best. "I submit to you that if a man hasn't discovered something he will die for, he isn't fit to live." Dr. Myles Munroe followed up nicely when he declared, "The only thing worse than death is life without purpose."

I've often told people that if they chase passion and purpose, then money, and everything else they desire, will find them. My purpose is to educate, equip, and empower people to reach their destiny by helping them to maximize their potential. That sounds great, and it is, but I didn't discover it automatically. I had to ask myself five questions of the heart—queries originally introduced by Dr. Munroe that will absolutely change your life and position you for ongoing success Saturday and every day.

Let's take a deeper dive into each one.

Heart question #1. Who am I?
This speaks to your identity. Many people want to be something that they are not, but we must be _____ with ourselves and come to know who we are not—and who we are. This requires looking at our talents and gifts to determine what gives us energy and moves us in a positive direction.

It was in 2002 that I had a serious talk with myself. I was in my office at church and working in full-time ministry as a pastor. We had just purchased a new building and were doing alright, but we had been through some struggles, and I was at a crossroads. At the core of my dilemma was a simple question: "Am I supposed to be doing this?"

I had friends who were running companies. Several of my former college classmates were doing well and producing products. They were achieving more things, had more money, and were getting more accolades, and that frustrated me. I felt left out. I was an engineer at General Motors. Yet I was stuck speaking to a hundred people every week at a church, and it seemed to me that I wasn't moving fast enough at all. *What was I doing being some ordinary preacher?* I mused. *I don't want to be an ordinary preacher.*

I discovered that morning that I actually didn't want to be like my friends or continue comparing myself to them based on their fame or the income they earned. I resolved that I didn't want to be a person who did what I did just for notoriety or for money. I ceased comparing myself to others and engaged my gifts in leadership. Essentially, I defined who I was, what I wanted to do, and why I wanted to do it at my heart level.

At the heart level, who are you? Answer as thoroughly as possible.

_____

_____

_____

_____

_____

Heart question #2. Where am I from?

This speaks to your source. We must determine the _____ of our passion and our position. Are they birthed from the books we read, the people we are around, a power higher than ourselves, or all of the above?

I was always a pretty smart guy, but I determined at General Motors that I was not going to rely on myself or my wits as the source of my promotion. My sources were going to be God, mentorship, and reading books on purpose and personal development, not just what I thought was best for me. I recognized that God had given me direction and the callings for my life, and I was going to constantly train, learn, and grow. I also went to several seminars offered by the company and outside groups.

As I acted intentionally and focused my mindset, I defined where I was from by identifying my sources and using them for education and inspiration.

At the heart level, where are you from? Answer as thoroughly as possible.

_____

_____

_____

_____

_____

Heart question #3. Why am I here?

This speaks to your purpose. It is essential to know why we exist. This includes a _____ of why we live in a certain area, why we move in certain circles, and why we are spurred to action by certain things.

This question is not answered overnight. It took me until I was 37 years of age to properly answer it. It came during my second trip to Nigeria. My first visit was solely to take part in an evangelical crusade, but this time I also conducted a leadership seminar under Dr. Timothy Ifedioranma. I felt energy and passion as I made my presentation, and I witnessed the positive effect it had on the participants. Not only were they excited, but they also asked some really tough questions. "Can you pastor and own a business?" "How do you lead in the business world versus the pastor's world?" They wanted to know more about what I did and when I was coming back.

That's when I knew that helping others maximize their potential defined the very heart of what I wanted to do.

At the heart level, why are you here? Answer as thoroughly as possible.

_____

_____

_____

_____

_____

Heart question #4. What can I do?

This speaks to your potential. We must ask ourselves what we can do in this world to "move the needle." That's a term that has been around for quite a while and calls to mind the volume gauge on an old radio or the needle on the speedometer of a classic car. Simply defined, to move the needle is to "change a situation to a noticeable degree." What gift do we _____ that can do this? Do we need to work harder, stay up later, or get up earlier to make it happen?

In 2011, I decided to live to my greatest potential. More specifically, I told myself I was going to "live full and die empty." I was in my early forties at the time, looking ahead to my fifties, and I was just beginning my leadership role at Ability Plus. I was chief operations officer then, and I observed that my style of leadership was having an impact on our employees, particularly those who had never before experienced leadership training. When I was all in, they were all in, and it caused them to head in a positive direction.

From then on, I started volunteering to serve on more director's boards and mentoring others even as I was being mentored. I also launched the API Institute of Leadership and Development, which offered seminars and training sessions to assist others in reaching their potential. I tell people that my plan is to work as hard as I can until I'm about 65 and then start backing off and enjoying other things. Whatever I do, work or leisure, I want to do it with my whole heart. When I close my eyes for good someday and go home to be with the Lord, I don't want to carry anything with me. I want to leave everything behind as a legacy to others.

At the heart level, what can you do? Answer as thoroughly as possible.

_____

_____

_____

_____

_____

Heart question #5. Where am I going?

This speaks to your destiny. What does the _____ look like?

Raised in government housing, I had to see beyond my neighborhood. Even as a kid, I saw people around me settling for less. When teenagers graduated from school, they might have gotten a job, but they weren't going to college or anywhere else. Mediocrity was fine with them. I didn't want any of that. I couldn't imagine being in my thirties and still living in a place, and in a system, where I had to do everything I could just to have food and housing.

In fifth grade, I made a decision: I was going to be successful. I looked into the future and saw a destiny where I owned a house and a car, ran businesses, and changed the world. I didn't know or understand how any of that would take place. I just envisioned it on the canvas of my imagination.

I did know that I was going to have to work hard and get good grades in school to make it possible, so I started applying myself and studying—and two teachers made an amazing difference that year. The first was Ms. O'Shields. She was my math teacher, and she recognized early on that I had a high math IQ. In her wisdom, she told me to work at my own speed, and I finished the math book in one semester. I became a tutor to the other kids, and she gave me other math to do that was more advanced and not in the textbook.

Ms. O'Shields rewarded me by driving me home from school in her small, yellow sports car, often stopping for ice cream along the way. Ms. O'Shields spoke into my life, insisting that I could be whatever I wanted to be. I was just a boy, but she was a mentor and encourager.

The second was my science teacher, Mrs. Scott. She was one of those teachers who was very disciplined and demanded the same from her pupils. Every Thursday was test day, and if anyone failed, they got a paddling on Friday. I know that sounds very old school and even abusive today, but back then it was the norm. Students who routinely failed wore two pairs of pants to lessen the sting of the paddling, hoping their name wasn't going to be called.

One Friday early in the year, she called *my* name. I was such a good student the whole class almost stopped breathing. So did I.

I was the last person she paddled that day. "I failed the test?" I asked, confused.

"No," she said. "I already talked to your mom. You had an 89. You don't make 89s. You make 99s in my class. You are capable of that."

I never got paddled again.

Ms. O'Shields and Mrs. Scott set the stage for me to go on, get a scholarship and sponsorship to attend Kettering University, and excel as an adult. I didn't stay in the neighborhood. I did not settle for mediocrity. In my heart, I knew where I was going—and I got there!

At the heart level, where are you going? Answer as thoroughly as possible.

_____

_____

_____

_____

_____

Typically, Saturday is a day to get things done that you couldn't take care of Monday-Friday. Of course, being Saturday, you may not want to do those things. After all, the weekend has arrived. It's time to chill a bit, right?

So, to help you stay productive yet relaxed, Saturday comes with a couple of attributes to do just that.

Saturday is a source of enthusiasm.

Enthusiasm is a mental _____ of victory along the marathon course of your week. In their original Olympic Games, the Greeks had a race that was unique. In it, the winner was not the runner who finished first. It was the runner who finished with his torch still lit.[25] An excitement and fervor to do your tasks for the day, combined with a plan to get it done, will keep your flame burning and propel you to achieve some incredible things.

Author Irving Stone spent a lifetime studying greatness, writing novelized biographies of such men as Michelangelo and Vincent van Gogh. Stone was once asked if he had found a thread that runs through the lives of all these exceptional people. His response was enlightening.

"I write about people who sometime in their life...have a vision or dream of something that should be accomplished...and they go to work. They are beaten over the head, knocked down, vilified, and for years they get nowhere. But every time they're knocked down, they stand up. You cannot destroy these people. And at the end of their lives, they've accomplished some modest part of what they set out to do."[26]

RAYMOND'S STORY

Raymond has never lacked enthusiasm despite setbacks that could've smothered his intensity and eagerness as mastermind of an international syndicate of import and export operations. Plagued with post traumatic stress disorder from a series of shootings as a young man in which he was almost killed, Raymond can be as sly and manipulative as he is charming. Yet he remains exceptionally intelligent and highly driven, appearing to always be three steps ahead of his competitors. Though he functions with his own set of morals, Raymond is polite, kind, and caring toward people that he has known for an extended period of time, and his affable persona is almost always on display.

He is also unfailingly compassionate and fiercely loyal to his family and others close to him. Much of his fervor for living comes from the love and support of his wife, Katarina, and his daughter, Lizzie. It is from them that he receives his unbreakable resilience and to them that he credits the positive aspects of his complicated character. Without them, Raymond insists he would not be the man he is today.

"You can't judge a book by its cover," he says of his own life's narrative, "but you can by its first few chapters, and certainly by its last."

Questions for application:

1. What setbacks do you have to face and overcome to have and maintain enthusiasm in your professional and personal life?

_____

_____

_____

_____

2. Who has the most positive impact in your life? How does that person fuel your zest for living?

_____

_____

_____

_____

3. What can you do, using the many suggestions from earlier in *No Bad Days*, to feed and nurture enthusiasm every Saturday?

_____

_____

_____

_____

_____

Saturday is the womb of perseverance.

Perseverance is having steady persistence in spite of difficulties or obstacles. On Saturday, this usually means pushing through and getting it done when distractions come upon you. It can also require you to _____ discouragement from others.

Even the greatest personalities have been told they wouldn't persevere or succeed. Former British statesman and prime minister Winston Churchill seemed so dull as a youth that his father thought he might be incapable of even earning a living in England. Writer and theologian G.K. Chesterton could not read until he was eight. One of his teachers cruelly told him, "If we could open your head, we should not find any brain but only a lump of white fat." Inventor Thomas Edison's first teacher described him as "addled," and his father almost convinced him he was a dunce. Theoretical physicist Albert Einstein, whose very name is synonymous with genius, performed so badly in all high school courses except mathematics that a teacher asked him to drop out.[27]

I'm so glad Ms. O'Shields and Mrs. Scott weren't like those teachers. Comments like this would have destroyed my perseverance before it could be birthed and grown.

MEGAN'S STORY

Megan is a first responder who learned perseverance not from a colleague, but from her nanny.

Born in the former Soviet Union at the start of the final decade of the Cold War, Masha Koslov grew up in near-poverty but developed a tireless work ethic and nurturing heart as a nanny, first to her own siblings as a girl and then for other families as a young adult. Masha immigrated to the United States in 2004, three years after Megan was born. Masha met Megan's parents at church just after her arrival. They befriended Masha, and she quickly connected with little Megan.

Since they both worked in high tech careers, Megan's parents hired Masha as a full-time, live-in nanny when Megan was five—and the two became inseparable. Megan was not only interested in Masha's stories about her childhood, but she was also fascinated by how Masha stood firm and kept going forward while living in a Communist regime and then transitioning out of one in the early 1990s.

When Megan began training to become a certified first responder, it was challenging. But Masha, who by then had become like a big sister to her, not only helped Megan study, but she continued to model perseverance to the now-young woman who she used to play Barbies with. Today, Masha is in her mid-forties and continues to take care of children. Megan spends time with her every weekend. "Quoting one of her favorite American actresses, Gillian Anderson, Masha always told me, 'Just remember, you can do anything you set your mind to, but it takes action, perseverance, and facing your fears," Megan said. "It's so true!"

Questions for application:

1. How have you learned perseverance from your own experiences growing up?

\
\
\
\
\

2. Masha was and remains Megan's role model. Who is yours, and what have they taught you about never giving up?

\
\
\
\
\

3. What can you apply from our earlier lessons on visualization to feed and nurture perseverance every Saturday?

\
\
\
\

Purposeful traits for a Successful Saturday

Eight is great, or so it is said—and over the years, I have identified and practiced eight traits that are ideal for nurturing direction and purpose on Saturday that will provide a foundation for your daily success.

Interestingly, each one requires selflessness and intentionality.

1. **Clearly communicate your vision and performance expectations.**

    On Saturday morning, I get up, make a cup of coffee, have a time of devotion reflecting on God's goodness, then go over my vision. As I do this each week, I look back at what was accomplished to get me that much closer to achieving the milestones and goals of the overall vision.

    One such morning in June 2019, I started my Successful Saturday routine and discovered that I was not putting enough focus on self-discipline. I was taking part in too many nonproductive meetings. So, I began streamlining my schedule to get rid of meetings that did not positively feed the future of the overall vision. Since then, I am more productive. I don't have wasted time. I look at my schedule, discern what is truly needed, and tell my administrative assistant to decline what's left. I've learned the power of delegation and the freedom that comes from saying "no." I can pass it on or refuse it, and it's okay.

    Remove any and all _____, then review your vision weekly, communicate it again to yourself, and do whatever is necessary to fulfill it.

    Right now, pick a day each week that you will recite and reflect on your vision. Write it down here, and place it in your schedule.

    _____

2. **Make lightning-fast decisions.**

    It's proper to take some time to ruminate and deliberate, but when the time for action arrives, stop _____ and go on.

    An often-used quote for business and inspiration states that while an open mind is priceless, "it is priceless only when its owner has the courage to make a final decision which closes the mind for action after the process of viewing all sides of the question has been completed. Failure to make a decision after due consideration of all the facts will quickly brand a man as unfit for a position of responsibility."

    It concludes, "Not all of your decisions will be correct. None of us is perfect. But if you get into the habit of making decisions, experience will develop your judgment to a point where it is better to be right fifty percent of the time and get something done, than it is to get nothing done because you fear to reach a decision."[28]

    Don't allow anxiety or concern to make you indecisive. Have confidence in your acquired wisdom and trust your instincts. Act—then proactively respond to whatever comes next.

157

HARRY'S STORY

In his role at the National Security Agency / Central Security Service of the United States government, Harry often has to make quick decisions. While he cannot share specific details about his work, Harry has made it clear that there are times when thoughtful analysis must be followed by decisive action. Cybersecurity alone prevents and eradicates threats to U.S. national security systems with a focus on the defense industrial base and the improvement of U.S. weapons' security—and that's just one facet of what that government agency oversees and protects.

Understandably, Harry brings that definitive decision making attitude home with him in his greater roles as husband to his wife, Charlene, and their two children. It is there, though, that he benefits from his spouse's wisdom and insights, and they call the shots as a couple on everything from daily interactions with their kids to weekly spending choices. The ability to come together in agreement, compromise when necessary, and act in one accord to find resolutions is invaluable to him and his family.

Harry treasures his wife's words about him. "The measure of a man is not how he behaves in moments of comfort and convenience," she said, "but how he stands at times of controversy and challenges."

Questions for application:

1. Describe how you have to be consistently decisive at your workplace.

_____

_____

_____

_____

_____

2. What do you have to regularly nurture about yourself so that you can continue to make quick decisions when necessary? Explain.

_____

_____

_____

_____

_____

3. Who has or does share the load with you in your decision making? Share how that person helps you the most.

_____

_____

_____

_____

_____

3. **Put the spotlight on others.**

Many times, it's easy to feel like no one is noticing what we're doing—but really, it's all about telling someone else's story anyway. I'm a big college football fan. On fall and winter Saturdays, ESPN's College GameDay spotlights athletes who have overcome adversity or done outstanding things for others and the communities where they play. These features go beyond the game and spotlight worthy young men and women.

Saturday is a great day for you to shine a light on somebody else just like ESPN does. That's why I usually call someone on my staff and tell them, "You know what so-and-so is doing? Let me tell you!" I declare how that individual has gone above and beyond to other leaders on my team. Many times, the person I feature is doing things others are not even aware of.

When you recognize and celebrate the success of others, it gives you a sense of _____ and even victory. When you see others who are winning, it opens your mind to doing the same thing yourself. It's a win-win for everyone!

Who in your life has done something incredible this week? Tell their story.

_____

_____

_____

_____

_____

4. Put yourself last.

Every young student knows of Isaac Newton's famed encounter with a falling apple. Newton discovered and introduced the laws of gravity in the 1600s, which revolutionized astronomical studies. But few know that if it weren't for Edmund Halley, the world might never have learned from Newton.

It was Halley who challenged Newton to think through his original notions. Halley corrected Newton's mathematical errors and prepared geometrical figures to support his discoveries. Halley coaxed the hesitant Newton to write his great work, *Philosophiæ Naturalis Principia Mathematica*, or Mathematical Principles of Natural Philosophy, first published in Latin in 1687. It was Halley who edited and supervised the publication and financed its printing.

Historians still refer to it as one of the most selfless examples in the annals of science. Newton began to reap the rewards of prominence almost immediately, and Halley received little credit. However, he did use the principles to predict the orbit and return of the comet that would later bear his name, but it was only after his death that Halley received any acclaim. Halley remained a devoted scientist who didn't care who received the credit as long as the cause was being advanced.[29]

Advancement solely for the sake of _____ is never a trait of a successful person. Use your gifts and talents to their fullest and to attain the greatest, regardless of recognition.

SUSAN'S STORY

Never comfortable in the limelight, Susan is a behind-the-scenes sort of person. Therefore, she's ideal for her career as a cleaner hired to come into a variety of settings to remediate and remove bodily fluids and other potentially hazardous materials. It is anything but easy and often unpleasant. Susan has worked on incidents ranging from accidents, suicide or attempted suicide, and homicides to industrial accidents, infectious disease contamination, and even animal biohazard contamination. It's a vocation few people dare to venture into.

Yet Susan says she wouldn't want to do anything else. "Being a cleaner gives me a unique view of life. I have routinely seen how life comes to an end. It is often tragic and always brutally harsh. But it has certainly caused me to understand the fragility of humans and the preciousness of a human life. Every day I have is precious, and every one is to be valued and lived in the moment."

With that mindset, it's not surprising, then, that Susan is enormously successful. She has earned national awards of merit for the quality of her work, and she has pioneered cleaning techniques that have set new standards of excellence in her field.

Questions for application:

1. In what ways has Susan put herself last in her chosen profession?

_____

_____

_____

_____

_____

2. When have you had to do something that few others wanted to do?

_____

_____

_____

_____

_____

3. What perspectives did you gain from that experience that informs how you view success?

_____

_____

_____

_____

_____

5. **Accept full responsibility and share the credit.**

We must accept the fact that 100 percent of what happens to us, or in the spaces where we lead, is our responsibility. This is true no matter how much or how little we can control and whether or not we win or lose. In addition, when triumphs occur, we should always share the credit with our team and anyone else who contributed to the victory.

When we landed a new client, the University of Alabama at Birmingham Health Systems, to receive coaching and leadership training, I told my team that it happened because of all of their hard work that resulted in the research and negotiating that secured the client. I credited them and rewarded them.

Conversely, when we fail, we must accept the fault as our own. When I made strategic changes in how the ministry and outreach of my church was conducted, we lost many people. At one point, it appeared we may have to close our doors entirely. I was the leader. I took the blame. I took responsibility for it. I could've blamed some of the members and volunteers at the church, but I put it on me and told everyone I was going to correct it. The strategic changes I made weren't wrong, and they weren't a failure. It was a transition that temporarily had negative consequences. Then, when things turned around, I gave credit to those who made it possible.

Never shirk your _____ and never think you're the only one running the show. Have the tenacity and courage to truly lead.

On a scale of 1-10 (with 10 being the highest), how do you rate your ability to accept responsibility for your actions?

_____

Why did you give yourself that score?

_____

_____

_____

_____

_____

6. **Keep people on their toes.**

Keeping others on their toes is simply the art of encouraging someone to take those few more steps to get to greatness. Many times on Saturday, I will take the time to ask one of my leaders if they have maximized their potential. Is there another step they can take on the ladder? Are they sure they are reaching for their best? Most of them thank me later for stretching them beyond what they thought was the maximum they could achieve.

One of our church leaders volunteers in our technology department, and he faced a huge personal challenge when we converted from an analog control board to a digital one for the building's audio, video, web services, and lighting. He was accustomed to the analog equipment and uncomfortable with learning the newer and more complex computerized system. "I'm going to need some help," he pleaded with me. "I don't know these computers."

I replied, "You can do it. It is in you. The skill set is already there. Now is the time to develop it like never before." He agreed to try. He failed a few times at first, but he persevered. Before long, he ran the digital system as well as the old analog one. Lighting, audio, video, webcasting—he could do it all.

Challenge _____ and be willing to have yourself and those you lead take on new things. Keep everyone on their toes and encourage them along the way.

Who can you encourage today? Name that person, and write down what you will say to them.

_____

_____

_____

_____

_____

7. **Take risks without being reckless.**

In 1982, the ABC Evening News reported on an unusual work of modern art—a chair affixed to a shotgun. It was to be viewed by sitting in the chair and looking directly into the gun barrel. The gun was loaded and set on a timer to fire at an undetermined moment within the next 100 years. The amazing thing was that people waited in lines to sit and stare into the shell's path! They all knew the gun could go off at point-blank range at any moment, but they were gambling that the fatal blast wouldn't happen during their minute in the chair.[30]

The risk they took with their lives was needless, but necessary risk is always a trait of a successful person. Former president Franklin D. Roosevelt once said, "It is common sense to take a method and try it. If it fails, admit it frankly. But above all, try something!" Failing to try because of a desire to be _____ results in inaction.

Take a chance, embrace calculated risk, and see what happens. A *No Bad Days* life is one that is fully lived!

AMIR'S STORY

Amir prefers to feel secure. Born in New England as the son of immigrants, Amir is a highly intelligent individual. He speaks several languages, and he mastered advanced calculus before he started middle school. But he is also anxious. He kids (or, at least, most people believe he is kidding) that he has spent his grandparent's inheritance on therapy.

His studies at the Massachusetts Institute of Technology resulted in Amir becoming a computer programmer, and he excels at his work. It isn't unusual for him to have to take risk as he troubleshoots complex fixes to the vast network of desktops, laptops, and tablets his employer requires—and each risk is a challenge for him, heightening his anxiety. But Amir presses in and through them by relying on his expertise and trusting in his intuition to take the necessary steps in a precise and orderly fashion. It is impossible for Amir to be reckless, yet inaction is also not an option.

Naturally introverted, Amir appreciates it when he receives recognition from his colleagues for his work on their behalf, though he remains shy and humble about it. Amir often quotes his favorite actor, Tom Baker, who portrayed the fourth doctor in the classic *Doctor Who* television series. Regarding praise, Baker stated, "I think if more people had more applause, it would make them feel better. I often give my wife a round of applause. If the meal is very good, I give her a standing ovation."

Questions for application:

1. When was the last time you had to embrace calculated risk? Tell the story.

2. How does anxiety typically come into play in your professional life?

3. Is there someone at your workplace like Amir who could use a round of applause from you? How would recognizing that person's accomplishments on your behalf make you feel?

_____

_____

_____

_____

_____

8. **Lead by example.**

One particularly inspiring tale of example, especially when you consider its historical context, occurred in 1865. One Sunday morning, a black man entered a fashionable church in Richmond, Virginia. When Communion was served, he walked down the aisle and knelt at the altar.

A rustle of resentment swept through the congregation. How dare he! After all, believers in that church used the common cup.

Suddenly, a distinguished layman stood up, stepped forward to the altar, and knelt beside the black man. With Robert E. Lee setting the example, the rest of the congregation soon followed his lead.[31]

Being a good example to others often requires _____, but it is worth it. Each Saturday, examine how you can be a better example to your family, friends, and colleagues—then follow through on that the rest of the week.

On a scale of 1-10 (with 10 being the highest), how do you rate your ability to lead by example?

_____

Why did you give yourself that score?

_____

_____

_____

_____

_____

Three principles of purpose

We've covered so much in *No Bad Days*, so it seems more than appropriate to close with three brief but incredible and foundational principles that will not only shine purpose into your Successful Saturdays, but every other day of the week as well.

Purpose is the master of motivation.

Motivation is the general desire or willingness to do something. An irresistible, consuming purpose will _____ you and will not let you go. Identify a purpose with goals that you've just got to reach. Then build toward those goals under the fire of anticipation.

Purpose is the mother of commitment.

Commitment is a deliberated and calculated choice to steadfastly set your course with an unwavering obligation to go above and beyond your original _____ to accomplish a predetermined objective.

Purpose gives birth to hope.

Hope is a feeling of expectation and desire for a certain thing to happen. Hope builds your self-confidence and inspires you to believe that you are _____ of achieving great things by enabling yourself to aim higher and work smarter.

Successful Saturday – Purpose **Fill-in-the-Blank Answer Key:**

honest	overcome	apathy
wellspring	distractions	secure
consideration	thinking	courage
possess	fulfillment	motivate
future	self	expectation
position	responsibility	capable

DON'T WAIT FOR TOMORROW!

As with most things in life, it all comes down to how you look at it.

Do you automatically think Monday will be a bad day, Wednesday will be a get-through-it sort of day, and Friday will be a great day? That's what most people tend to believe.

But that's just it: it's a belief based on a preconception. Therefore, if you begin to believe that every day will be a great day filled with productivity and joy—that there are indeed *No Bad Days*—guess what that does to your attitude? It transforms it!

That mindset change is essential, but it is not enough. You need to follow it up with action, and that is what *No Bad Days* empowers you to do. It gives you principles and calls to action that you can implement every day.

"Thank God it's Friday?" Maybe. But how about if you can start to say, "Thank God it's Monday, or Tuesday, or Wednesday"—or whatever day it is? There are opportunities in every day. No matter the circumstances, no matter how hard it is, and no matter how tough it seems, it doesn't make a difference! Why? You are not living for the weekend. You are living for each day as it comes!

What has writing and living *No Bad Days* done to me? It calls upon me to not wait for tomorrow to have joy. It calls upon me to approach every day with the idea that I can accomplish something. When I get up in the morning, it is the first day of the rest of my life! It forces me to maximize that day so that I can leave it all on the field and get the most out of it.

Tomorrow will take care of itself. It might have problems. It might have challenges. But I will not wait until tomorrow to experience my fullest life today!

Can you think of any better way to live than that?

Monitor each day of the week, according to each day's theme, for two weeks. Be sure to note your mindset and actions for each day.

_____

_____

_____

_____

_____

_____

_____

_____

_____

_____

_____

_____

ENDNOTES

1   Martin Luther King, Jr., "I Have A Dream: Writings and Speeches that Changed the World," ed. James Melvin Washington (San Francisco: Harper, 1986), pgs. 102-106.

2   Robert J. Morgan, Nelson's Annual Preacher's Sourcebook, 2002 Edition, (Thomas Nelson Inc., 2001), p.324.

3   https://theanguillian.com/2017/11/from-rags-to-riches-the-life-story-of-dr-myles-munroe-by-russel-reid/

4   "Researcher: Monday Funk All in the Mind," Chicago Tribune, July 2, 1997, sec. 1, pg. 8.

5   Let's Be: The power of thoughts. The Express, by Nancy Hackenberg, certified life coach and owner of Be One Healthy Fitness Center, Mill Hall, PA. https://www.lockhaven.com/news/health-and-home/2022/03/lets-be-the-power-of-thoughts/

6   Learning to Lead, J.M. Boice, Revell, 1990, p. 38. Taken from http://www.sermonillustrations.com/

7   Mike Lupica in Esquire. Taken from http://www.sermonillustrations.com/

8   Bits & Pieces, September 19, 1991, p. 9. Taken from http://www.sermonillustrations.com/

9   John McKay, "A Coach's Story." Taken from http://www.sermonillustrations.com/

10 https://kclpure.kcl.ac.uk/portal/robert.plomin.html

11 Source Unknown. Taken from http://www.sermonillustrations.com/

12 William C. Schultz, Bits & Pieces, December 1990. Taken from http://www.sermonillustrations.com/

13 Today in the Word, September 5, 1993. Taken from http://www.sermonillustrations.com/

14 Our Daily Bread. Taken from http://www.sermonillustrations.com/

15 Bits and Pieces, November, 1989, p. 21. Taken from http://www.sermonillustrations.com/

16 M. Littleton in Moody Monthly, June, 1989, p. 29. Taken from http://www.sermonillustrations.com/

17 Bits & Pieces, June 24, 1993, pp. 20-21. Taken from http://www.sermonillustrations.com/

18 Bits and Pieces, June 25, 1992. Taken from http://www.sermonillustrations.com/

19 Swindoll, The Quest For Character, Multnomah, p. 62-3. Taken from http://www.sermonillustrations.com/

20 Beals, Beyond Hunger. Taken from http://www.sermonillustrations.com/

21 Today in the Word, July, 1990, p. 17. Taken from http://www.sermonillustrations.com/

22 Harry Heintz. Taken from http://www.sermonillustrations.com/

23 Dr. Maxwell Maltz, quoted in Bits & Pieces, June 24, 1993, p. 12. Taken from http://www.sermonillustrations.com/

24 Zaida Jones Blaine in Chicago Tribune. Taken from http://www.sermonillustrations.com/

25 J. Stowell, Fan The Flame, Moody, 1986, p. 32. Taken from http://www.sermonillustrations.com/

26 Crossroads, Issue No. 7, p. 18. Taken from http://www.sermonillustrations.com/

27 Irving Wallace, Book of Lists, 1986, Wm. Morrow & Co., Ny, Ny. Taken from http://www.
    sermonillustrations.com/

28 Taken from http://www.sermonillustrations.com/

29 C.S. Kirkendall, Jr. Taken from http://www.sermonillustrations.com/

30 Jeffrey D. King. Taken from http://www.sermonillustrations.com/

31 Today in the Word, September, 1991, p. 15. Taken from http://www.sermonillustrations.com/

www.ingramcontent.com/pod-product-compliance
Lightning Source LLC
Chambersburg PA
CBHW080841120626
46553CB00009B/2526